A Bible Treasury

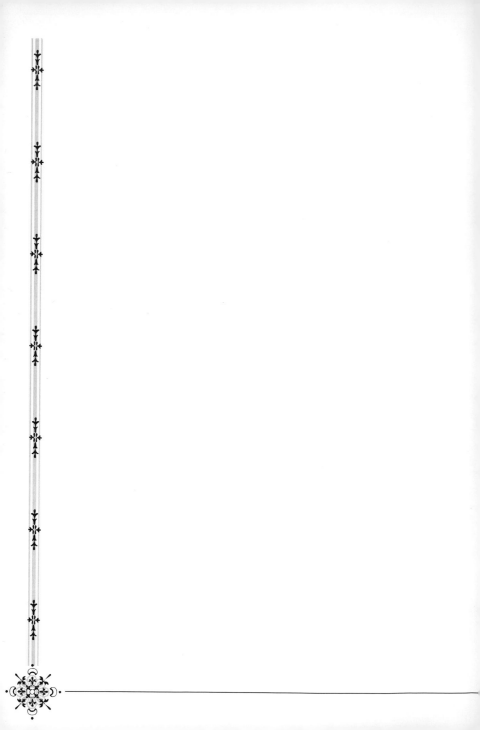

This edition copyright © 1998 Lion Publishing

Published by
Lion Publishing plc
Sandy Lane West, Oxford, England
www.lion-publishing.co.uk
ISBN 0 7459 3934 1
First edition 1998
10 9 8 7 6 5 4

A catalogue record for this book is available
from the British Library

Printed and bound in Singapore

A Bible Treasury

A LION BOOK

CONTENTS

PART ONE: OLD TESTAMENT

Part Two: New Testament

INTRODUCTION

The Bible is one of the world's bestsellers. Within its covers people from many and varied backgrounds have found inspiration, guidance, comfort and encouragement throughout the ages. Indeed, numerous images and phrases from the Bible have passed into the English language and are a rich part of our heritage.

The Bible is a treasure house of many different types of literature, written for differing purposes. The passages in this *Bible Treasury* have been chosen to represent this variety of writings, and are drawn from a number of different translations. Here, from the Authorized Version, is the inspiring Sermon on the Mount from Matthew's gospel; the 23rd Psalm, 'The Lord is My Shepherd'; Saint Luke's account of the birth of Jesus, complete with shepherds and angels; and many others. A number of different translations have been used for other passages, for sometimes a familiar passage can be seen in an entirely new way in a new translation. Each passage has a short introduction to help set the scene, or put the passage in context.

Although the Bible is one 'book', it is made up of different kinds of smaller books, but taken as a whole, they all tell one great story – of God, who made the world, and of his love for his creation. The Old Testament is the story of God's 'chosen' people, the Israelites. It includes history, laws, poetry, wise sayings and the words of the prophets. The New Testament, written after the time of Jesus, tells of his life, death and resurrection in the four gospels, and then goes on to show how the first Christians understood the message Jesus had brought

9

and started spreading the 'good news'. The New Testament finishes with John's extraordinary vision of 'a new heaven and a new earth' in the Book of Revelation.

The Bible is about real people – wise, foolish, wicked, virtuous, faithful, faithless, sad, joyful – there are no bounds to the human experience portrayed here! Their stories give the Bible its timeless appeal. And the one thread which links them all is the theme of God the creator, sustainer, judge and saviour, most completely revealed in Jesus.

Pope Gregory the Great, who was instrumental in sending Augustine to England with the 'good news' said, 'The Bible is like a wide river in which lambs may splash in the shallows and elephants may swim to their hearts' content.' If you are someone who already enjoys soaking in the vast riches of the Bible's resources, may you find the different translations used here new and stimulating. And if you are familiar with only a few of the passages in this *Bible Treasury*, may you begin to enjoy more of this greatest of books.

PART ONE

THE OLD TESTAMENT

THE STORY OF CREATION

The first book of the Bible, the book of Genesis, is a book of beginnings. Here is an account of the beginning of our world, a mystical and evocative telling which places God firmly at the centre of all creation.

In the beginning God created the heaven and the earth. And the earth was without form, and void; and darkness was upon the face of the deep. And the Spirit of God moved upon the face of the waters.

And God said, Let there be light: and there was light. And God saw the light, that it was good: and God divided the light from the darkness. And God called the light Day, and the darkness he called Night. And the evening and the morning were the first day.

And God said, Let there be a firmament in the midst of the waters, and let it divide the waters from the waters. And God made the firmament, and divided the waters which were under the firmament from the waters which were above the firmament: and it was so. And God called the firmament Heaven. And the evening and the morning were the second day.

And God said, Let the waters under the heaven be gathered together unto one place, and let the dry land appear: and it was so. And God called the dry land Earth; and the gathering together of the waters called he Seas: and God saw that it was good. And God said, Let the earth bring forth grass, the herb yielding seed, and the fruit tree yielding fruit after his kind, whose seed is in itself, upon the earth: and it was so. And the earth brought forth grass, and herb yielding seed after his kind, and the tree yielding fruit, whose seed was in itself, after his kind: and God saw that it was good. And the evening and the morning were the third day.

And God said, Let there be lights in the firmament of the heaven to divide the day from the night; and let them be for signs, and for seasons, and for days, and years: and let them be for lights in the firmament of the heaven to give light upon the earth: and it was so. And God made two great lights; the greater light to rule the day, and the lesser light to rule the night: he made the stars also. And God set them in the firmament of the heaven to give light upon the earth, and to rule over the day and over the night, and to divide the light from the darkness: and God saw that it was good. And the evening and the morning were the fourth day.

And God said, Let the waters bring forth abundantly the moving creature that hath life, and fowl that may fly above the earth in the open firmament of heaven. And God created great whales, and every living creature that moveth, which the waters brought forth abundantly, after their kind, and every winged fowl after his kind: and God saw that it was good. And God blessed them, saying, Be fruitful, and multiply, and fill the waters in the seas, and let fowl multiply in the earth. And the evening and the morning were the fifth day.

And God said, Let the earth bring forth the living creature after his kind, cattle, and creeping thing, and beast of the earth after his kind: and it was so. And God made the beast of the earth after his kind, and cattle after their kind, and every thing that creepeth upon the earth after his kind: and God saw that it was good. And God said, Let us make man in our image, after our likeness: and let them have dominion over the fish of the sea, and over the fowl of the air, and over the cattle, and over all the earth, and over every creeping thing that creepeth

13

upon the earth. So God created man in his own image, in the image of God created he him; male and female created he them. And God blessed them, and God said unto them, Be fruitful, and multiply, and replenish the earth, and subdue it: and have dominion over the fish of the sea, and over the fowl of the air, and over every living thing that moveth upon the earth. And God said, Behold, I have given you every herb bearing seed, which is upon the face of all the earth, and every tree, in the which is the fruit of a tree yielding seed; to you it shall be for meat. And to every beast of the earth, and to every fowl of the air, and to every thing that creepeth upon the earth, wherein there is life, I have given every green herb for meat: and it was so. And God saw every thing that he had made, and, behold, it was very good. And the evening and the morning were the sixth day.

Thus the heavens and the earth were finished, and all the host of them. And on the seventh day God ended his work which he had made; and he rested on the seventh day from all his work which he had made. And God blessed the seventh day, and sanctified it: because that in it he had rested from all his work which God created and made.

FROM THE BOOK OF GENESIS, CHAPTERS 1 AND 2

14

THE GARDEN OF EDEN

The pinnacle of God's creation is humankind, made in God's own image to love and be loved by God. The very first people, Adam and Eve, were placed in a 'garden' of perfect beauty and balance: the Garden of Eden.

These are the generations of the heavens and of the earth when they were created, in the day that the Lord God made the earth and the heavens, and every plant of the field before it was in the earth, and every herb of the field before it grew: for the Lord God had not caused it to rain upon the earth, and there was not a man to till the ground. But there went up a mist from the earth, and watered the whole face of the ground. And the Lord God formed man of the dust of the ground, and breathed into his nostrils the breath of life; and man became a living soul.

And the Lord God planted a garden eastward in Eden; and there he put the man whom he had formed. And out of the ground made the Lord God to grow every tree that is pleasant to the sight, and good for food; the tree of life also in the midst of the garden, and the tree of knowledge of good and evil…

And the Lord God took the man, and put him into the garden of Eden to dress it and to keep it. And the Lord God commanded the man, saying, Of every tree of the garden thou mayest freely eat: but of the tree of the knowledge of good and evil, thou shalt not eat of it: for in the day that thou eatest thereof thou shalt surely die.

And the Lord God said, It is not good that the man should

be alone; I will make him an help meet for him. And out of the ground the Lord God formed every beast of the field, and every fowl of the air; and brought them unto Adam to see what he would call them: and whatsoever Adam called every living creature, that was the name thereof.

And Adam gave names to all cattle, and to the fowl of the air, and to every beast of the field; but for Adam there was not found an help meet for him. And the Lord God caused a deep sleep to fall upon Adam, and he slept: and he took one of his ribs, and closed up the flesh instead thereof; and the rib, which the Lord God had taken from man, made he a woman, and brought her unto the man. And Adam said, This is now bone of my bones, and flesh of my flesh: she shall be called Woman, because she was taken out of Man. Therefore shall a man leave his father and his mother, and shall cleave unto his wife: and they shall be one flesh. And they were both naked, the man and his wife, and were not ashamed.

FROM THE BOOK OF GENESIS, CHAPTER 2

16

THE FALL

For God's people to be truly a reflection of God himself, and not mere puppets, they had to be able to make their own choices – to have a free will. The story of 'the fall' is the story of how Adam and Eve made the choice to ignore God's directions, and the consequences of that choice.

Now the serpent was more subtil than any beast of the field which the Lord God had made. And he said unto the woman, Yea, hath God said, Ye shall not eat of every tree of the garden?

And the woman said unto the serpent, We may eat of the fruit of the trees of the garden: but of the fruit of the tree which is in the midst of the garden, God hath said, Ye shall not eat of it, neither shall ye touch it, lest ye die. And the serpent said unto the woman, Ye shall not surely die: For God doth know that in the day ye eat thereof, then your eyes shall be opened, and ye shall be as gods, knowing good and evil.

And when the woman saw that the tree was good for food, and that it was pleasant to the eyes, and a tree to be desired to make one wise, she took of the fruit thereof, and did eat, and gave also unto her husband with her; and he did eat. And the eyes of them both were opened, and they knew that they were naked; and they sewed fig leaves together, and made themselves aprons.

And they heard the voice of the Lord God walking in the garden in the cool of the day: and Adam and his wife hid themselves from the presence of the Lord God amongst the

17

trees of the garden. And the Lord God called unto Adam, and said unto him, Where art thou? And he said, I heard thy voice in the garden, and I was afraid, because I was naked; and I hid myself.

And he said, Who told thee that thou wast naked? Hast thou eaten of the tree, whereof I commanded thee that thou shouldest not eat?

And the man said, The woman whom thou gavest to be with me, she gave me of the tree, and I did eat.

And the Lord God said unto the woman, What is this that thou hast done? And the woman said, The serpent beguiled me, and I did eat.

And the Lord God said unto the serpent, Because thou hast done this, thou art cursed above all cattle, and above every beast of the field; upon thy belly shalt thou go, and dust shalt thou eat all the days of thy life: and I will put enmity between thee and the woman, and between thy seed and her seed; it shall bruise thy head, and thou shalt bruise his heel.

Unto the woman he said, I will greatly multiply thy sorrow and thy conception; in sorrow thou shalt bring forth children; and thy desire shall be to thy husband, and he shall rule over thee.

And unto Adam he said, Because thou hast hearkened unto the voice of thy wife, and hast eaten of the tree, of which I commanded thee, saying, Thou shalt not eat of it: cursed is the ground for thy sake; in sorrow shalt thou eat of it all the days of thy life; thorns also and thistles shall it bring forth to thee; and thou shalt eat the herb of the field; in the sweat of thy face shalt thou eat bread, till thou return unto the ground; for out of it wast thou taken: for dust thou art, and unto dust shalt thou return. And Adam called his wife's name Eve; because she was the mother of all living.

Unto Adam also and to his wife did the Lord God make coats

of skins, and clothed them. And the Lord God said, Behold, the man is become as one of us, to know good and evil: and now, lest he put forth his hand, and take also of the tree of life, and eat, and live for ever: therefore the Lord God sent him forth from the garden of Eden, to till the ground from whence he was taken. So he drove out the man; and he placed at the east of the garden of Eden cherubims, and a flaming sword which turned every way, to keep the way of the tree of life.

FROM THE BOOK OF GENESIS, CHAPTER 3

CAIN AND ABEL

Perhaps two of the most famous brothers in history are Cain and Abel. Their tragic and curious story, retold in the book of Genesis, is one of rivalry, fury and lies – and leads to God's retribution.

The man lay with his wife Eve, and she conceived and gave birth to Cain. She said, 'With the help of the Lord I have brought into being a male child.' Afterwards she had another child, Abel. He tended the flock, and Cain worked the land. In due season Cain brought some of the fruits of the earth as an offering to the Lord, while Abel brought the choicest of the firstborn of his flock. The Lord regarded Abel and his offering with favour, but not Cain and his offering. Cain was furious and he glowered. The Lord said to Cain,

'Why are you angry? Why are you scowling?
If you do well, you hold your head up;
if not, sin is a demon crouching at the door;
it will desire you, and you will be mastered by it.'

Cain said to his brother Abel, 'Let us go out into the country.' Once there, Cain attacked and murdered his brother. The Lord asked Cain, 'Where is your brother Abel?' 'I do not know,' Cain answered. 'Am I my brother's keeper?' The Lord said, 'What have you done? Your brother's blood is crying out to me from the ground. Now you are accursed and will be banished from the very ground which has opened its mouth to receive the blood you have shed. When you till the ground, it will no longer yield you its produce. You shall be a wanderer, a fugitive on the earth.'

Cain said to the Lord, 'My punishment is heavier than I can bear; now you are driving me off the land, and I must hide myself from your presence. I shall be a wanderer, a fugitive on the earth, and I can be killed at sight by anyone.' The Lord answered him, 'No: if anyone kills Cain, sevenfold vengeance will be exacted from him.' The Lord put a mark on Cain, so that anyone happening to meet him should not kill him. Cain went out from the Lord's presence and settled in the land of Nod to the east of Eden.

FROM THE BOOK OF GENESIS, CHAPTER 4

NOAH AND THE GREAT FLOOD

The story of Noah and the ark has transcended millennia, and remains a firm favourite with children and adults alike. Yet this is a serious story, an account both of God's righteous anger and his loving forgiveness – the story, indeed, of a new beginning.

This is the story of Noah. He had three sons, Shem, Ham, and Japheth. Noah had no faults and was the only good man of his time. He lived in fellowship with God, but everyone else was evil in God's sight, and violence had spread everywhere. God looked at the world and saw that it was evil, for the people were all living evil lives.

God said to Noah, 'I have decided to put an end to the whole human race. I will destroy them completely, because the world is full of their violent deeds. Build a boat for yourself out of good timber; make rooms in it and cover it with tar inside and out. Make it 133 metres long, 22 metres wide, and 13 metres high. Make a roof for the boat and leave a space of 44 centimetres between the roof and the sides. Build it with three decks and put a door in the side. I am going to send a flood on the earth to destroy every living being. Everything on earth will die, but I will make a covenant with you. Go into the boat with your wife, your sons, and their wives. Take into the boat with you a male and a female of every kind of animal and of every kind of bird, in order to keep them alive. Take along all kinds of food for you and for them. Noah did everything that God commanded...

When Noah was 600 years old, on the seventeenth day of the second month all the outlets of the vast body of water beneath the earth burst open, all the floodgates of the sky were opened, and rain fell on the earth for forty days and nights...

God had not forgotten Noah and all the animals with him in the boat; he caused a wind to blow, and the water started going down. The outlets of the water beneath the earth and the floodgates of the sky were closed. The rain stopped, and the water gradually went down for 150 days... By the twenty-seventh day of the second month the earth was completely dry.

God said to Noah, 'Go out of the boat with your wife, your sons, and their wives. Take all the birds and animals out with you, so that they may reproduce and spread all over the earth. So Noah went out of the boat with his wife, his sons, and their wives. All the animals and birds went out of the boat in groups of their own kind.

FROM THE BOOK OF GENESIS, CHAPTERS 6 AND 7

THE TOWER OF BABEL

In this famous Old Testament story, Noah's descendants travel to Babylonia and there embark upon a massive building project – a city with a tower 'with its top in the heavens'. Their plan comes to naught when they suddenly find they are speaking different languages.

And the whole earth was of one language, and of one speech. And it came to pass, as they journeyed from the east, that they found a plain in the land of Shinar; and they dwelt there.

And they said one to another, Go to, let us make brick, and burn them throughly. And they had brick for stone, and slime had they for mortar.

And they said, Go to, let us build us a city and a tower, whose top may reach unto heaven; and let us make us a name, lest we be scattered abroad upon the face of the whole earth.

And the Lord came down to see the city and the tower, which the children of men builded. And the Lord said, Behold, the people is one, and they have all one language; and this they begin to do: and now nothing will be restrained from them, which they have imagined to do. Go to, let us go down, and there confound their language, that they may not understand one another's speech.

So the Lord scattered them abroad from thence upon the face of all the earth: and they left off to build the city. Therefore is the name of it called Babel; because the Lord did there confound the language of all the earth: and from thence did the Lord scatter them abroad upon the face of all the earth.

FROM THE BOOK OF GENESIS, CHAPTER 11

24

Promise to Abraham

God promised Abram that he would become Abraham – 'the father of a multitude'. It looked impossible, for his wife Sarah was well past the age of child-bearing. But, years later, Abraham's faith was rewarded with the birth of Isaac.

The word of the Lord came to Abram in a vision, 'Do not be afraid, Abram, I am your shield; your reward shall be very great.' But Abram said, 'O Lord God, what will you give me, for I continue childless, and the heir of my house is Eliezer of Damascus?' And Abram said, 'You have given me no offspring, and so a slave born in my house is to be my heir.'

But the word of the Lord came to him, 'This man shall not be your heir; no one but your very own issue shall be your heir.' He brought him outside and said, 'Look towards heaven and count the stars, if you are able to count them.' Then he said to him, 'So shall your descendants be.'

And he believed the Lord; and the Lord reckoned it to him as righteousness.

FROM THE BOOK OF GENESIS, CHAPTER 15

25

ABRAHAM'S FAITH

*It was a miracle! Sarah had borne Abraham a child
when they were both old and grey. God had kept his
promise. This story is about a test of obedience – is
Abraham's faith in God strong enough to obey,
whatever the cost?*

After these things God tested Abraham. He said to him,
'Abraham!' And he said, 'Here I am.' He said, 'Take your son,
your only son Isaac, whom you love, and go to the land of Moriah,
and offer him there as a burnt-offering on one of the mountains
that I shall show you.'

So Abraham rose early in the morning, saddled his donkey, and
took two of his young men with him, and his son Isaac; he cut the
wood for the burnt-offering, and set out and went to the place in
the distance that God had shown him.

On the third day Abraham looked up and saw the place far
away. Then Abraham said to his young men, 'Stay here with the
donkey; the boy and I will go over there; we will worship, and then
we will come back to you.'

Abraham took the wood of the burnt-offering and laid it on his
son Isaac, and he himself carried the fire and the knife. So the two
of them walked on together.

Isaac said to his father Abraham, 'Father!' And he said, 'Here I
am, my son.' He said, 'The fire and the wood are here, but where
is the lamb for a burnt-offering?'

Abraham said, 'God himself will provide the lamb for a burnt-
offering, my son.' So the two of them walked on together.

When they came to the place that God had shown him,

Abraham built an altar there and laid the wood in order. He bound his son Isaac, and laid him on the altar, on top of the wood. Then Abraham reached out his hand and took the knife to kill his son. But the angel of the Lord called to him from heaven, and said, 'Abraham, Abraham!' And he said, 'Here I am.'

He said, 'Do not lay your hand on the boy or do anything to him; for now I know that you fear God, since you have not withheld your son, your only son, from me.'

And Abraham looked up and saw a ram, caught in a thicket by its horns. Abraham went and took the ram and offered it up as a burnt-offering instead of his son. So Abraham called that place 'The Lord will provide'; as it is said to this day, 'On the mount of the Lord it shall be provided.'

FROM THE BOOK OF GENESIS, CHAPTER 22

JACOB'S LADDER

*The promise of God to Abraham and his descendants
runs like a golden thread through the book of Genesis.
It is a gracious God who reveals himself to Jacob, a
man who has deceived his father, Isaac, and cheated
his brother and is now on the run.*

Jacob left Beersheba and started towards Haran. At sunset he
came to a holy place and camped there. He lay down to sleep,
resting his head on a stone.

He dreamt that he saw a stairway reaching from earth to
heaven, with angels going up and coming down on it. And there
was the Lord standing beside him. 'I am the Lord, the God of
Abraham and Isaac,' he said. 'I will give to you and to your
descendants this land on which you are lying. They will be as
numerous as the specks of dust on the earth. They will extend
their territory in all directions, and through you and your
descendants I will bless all the nations.

'Remember, I will be with you and protect you wherever you go,
and I will bring you back to this land. I will not leave you until I
have done all that I have promised you.'

Jacob woke up and said, 'The Lord is here! He is in this place,
and I didn't know it!'

He was afraid and said, 'What a terrifying place this is! It must
be the house of God; it must be the gate that opens into heaven.'

Jacob got up early next morning, took the stone that was under
his head, and set it up as a memorial. Then he poured olive-oil on
it to dedicate it to God.

FROM THE BOOK OF GENESIS, CHAPTER 28

A New Name

Jacob, now reconciled with the brother he cheated and having found peace with God, receives a new name. Jacob's twelve sons are to become the fathers of the twelve tribes of Israel. Bethel means 'the house of God'.

When Jacob returned from Mesopotamia, God appeared to him again and blessed him.

God said to him, 'Your name is Jacob, but from now on it will be Israel.' So God named him Israel.

And God said to him, 'I am Almighty God. Have many children. Nations will be descended from you, and you will be the ancestor of kings. I will give you the land which I gave to Abraham and to Isaac, and I will also give it to your descendants after you.' Then God left him.

There, where God had spoken to him, Jacob set up a memorial stone and consecrated it by pouring wine and olive-oil on it. He named the place Bethel.

FROM THE BOOK OF GENESIS, CHAPTER 35

Joseph

*Joseph, doted upon by an ageing father, was a young
man who had dreams of grandeur. Favouritism within a
family inevitably brings resentment. Here it gives rise to
attempted murder. Many years later God would bring
reconciliation to this broken family by most unusual
means.*

Because Joseph was a child of his old age, Israel loved him best
of all his sons, and he made him a long robe with sleeves.
When his brothers saw that their father loved him best, it aroused
their hatred and they had nothing but harsh words for him…

Joseph went after his brothers and came up with them at
Dothan. They saw him in the distance, and before he reached
them, they plotted to kill him. 'Here comes that dreamer,' they
said to one another. 'Now is our chance; let us kill him and throw
him into one of these cisterns; we can say that a wild beast has
devoured him. Then we shall see what becomes of his dreams.'

When Reuben heard, he came to his rescue, urging them not
to take his life. 'Let us have no bloodshed,' he said. 'Throw him
into this cistern in the wilderness, but do him no injury.' Reuben
meant to rescue him from their clutches in order to restore him to
his father. When Joseph reached his brothers, they stripped him of
the long robe with sleeves which he was wearing, picked him up,
and threw him into the cistern. It was empty, with no water in it.

They had sat down to eat when, looking up, they saw an
Ishmaelite caravan coming from Gilead on the way down to Egypt,
with camels carrying gum tragacanth and balm and myrrh. Judah
said to his brothers, 'What do we gain by killing our brother and

30

concealing his death? Why not sell him to these Ishmaelites? Let us do him no harm, for after all, he is our brother, our own flesh and blood'; his brothers agreed. Meanwhile some passing Midianite merchants drew Joseph up out of the cistern and sold him for twenty pieces of silver to the Ishmaelites; they brought Joseph to Egypt. When Reuben came back to the cistern, he found Joseph had gone. He tore his clothes and going to his brothers he said, 'The boy is not there. Whatever shall I do?'

Joseph's brothers took the long robe with sleeves, and dipped it in the blood of a goat which they had killed. After tearing the robe, they brought it to their father and said, 'Look what we have found. Do you recognize it? Is this your son's robe or not?' Jacob recognized it. 'It is my son's,' he said. 'A wild beast has devoured him. Joseph has been torn to pieces.'

Jacob tore his clothes; he put on sackcloth and for many days he mourned his son. Though his sons and daughters all tried to comfort him, he refused to be comforted. He said, 'No, I shall go to Sheol mourning for my son.' Thus Joseph's father wept for him. The Midianites meanwhile had sold Joseph in Egypt to Potiphar, one of Pharaoh's court officials, the captain of the guard.

FROM THE BOOK OF GENESIS, CHAPTER 37

31

THE BIRTH OF MOSES

*A Hebrew baby is rescued from the reeds by the side of
a river. The story is well-known, but it is by no means
sentimental: the baby has been hidden to escape death
by being thrown into the Nile, the fate Pharaoh has
pronounced on the male children of his Hebrew slaves.*

Now a man from the house of Levi went and married a Levite
woman. The woman conceived and bore a son; and when she
saw that he was a fine baby, she hid him for three months. When
she could hide him no longer she got a papyrus basket for him, and
plastered it with bitumen and pitch; she put the child in it and
placed it among the reeds on the bank of the river. His sister stood
at a distance, to see what would happen to him.

The daughter of Pharaoh came down to bathe at the river,
while her attendants walked beside the river. She saw the basket
among the reeds and sent her maid to bring it. When she opened
it, she saw the child. He was crying, and she took pity on him.
'This must be one of the Hebrews' children,' she said.

Then his sister said to Pharaoh's daughter, 'Shall I go and get
you a nurse from the Hebrew women to nurse the child for you?'
Pharaoh's daughter said to her, 'Yes.' So the girl went and called
the child's mother. Pharaoh's daughter said to her, 'Take this child
and nurse it for me, and I will give you your wages.' So the woman
took the child and nursed it.

When the child grew up, she brought him to Pharaoh's
daughter, and she took him as her son. She named him Moses,
'because', she said, 'I drew him out of the water.'

FROM THE BOOK OF EXODUS, CHAPTER 2

32

THE BURNING BUSH

*For generations God's people had suffered cruelty
and injustice at the hands of the Egyptians. Moses
has witnessed it all. Now in exile in the desert, perhaps
he feared that God had forgotten his people.*

Moses... came to Horeb, the mountain of God. There the angel of the Lord appeared to him in a flame of fire out of a bush; he looked, and the bush was blazing, yet it was not consumed. Then Moses said, 'I must turn aside and look at this great sight, and see why the bush is not burned up.' When the Lord saw that he had turned aside to see, God called to him out of the bush, 'Moses, Moses!' And he said, 'Here I am.' Then he said, 'Come no closer! Remove the sandals from your feet, for the place on which you are standing is holy ground.' He said further, 'I am the God of your father, the God of Abraham, the God of Isaac, and the God of Jacob.' And Moses hid his face, for he was afraid to look at God.

Then the Lord said, 'I have observed the misery of my people who are in Egypt; I have heard their cry on account of their taskmasters. Indeed, I know their sufferings, and I have come down to deliver them from the Egyptians, and to bring them up out of that land to a good and broad land, a land flowing with milk and honey, to the country of the Canaanites, the Hittites, the Amorites, the Perizzites, the Hivites, and the Jebusites. The cry of the Israelites has now come to me; I have also seen how the Egyptians oppress them. So come, I will send you to Pharaoh to bring my people, the Israelites, out of Egypt.'

FROM THE BOOK OF EXODUS, CHAPTER 3

THE NAME OF GOD

*'Why me?' It's a natural reaction to a challenge which
will involve courage, hardship and danger. Moses, like
most of us, feels unequal to the task. But God promises,
'I am with you'. And the rewards? A land 'flowing with
milk and honey'.*

And Moses said unto God, Who am I, that I should go unto
Pharaoh, and that I should bring forth the children of Israel
out of Egypt? And he said, Certainly I will be with thee; and this
shall be a token unto thee, that I have sent thee: when thou hast
brought forth the people out of Egypt, ye shall serve God upon this
mountain.

And Moses said unto God, Behold, when I come unto the
children of Israel, and shall say unto them, The God of your
fathers hath sent me unto you; and they shall say to me, What
is his name? what shall I say unto them?

And God said unto Moses, I AM THAT I AM: and he said,
Thus shalt thou say unto the children of Israel, I AM hath sent me
unto you.

And God said moreover unto Moses, Thus shalt thou say unto
the children of Israel, The Lord God of your fathers, the God of
Abraham, the God of Isaac, and the God of Jacob, hath sent me
unto you: this is my name for ever, and this is my memorial unto
all generations. Go, and gather the elders of Israel together, and
say unto them, The Lord God of your fathers, the God of Abraham,
of Isaac, and of Jacob, appeared unto me, saying, I have surely
visited you, and seen that which is done to you in Egypt: and I
have said, I will bring you up out of the affliction of Egypt

unto the land of the Canaanites, and the Hittites, and the Amorites, and the Perizzites, and the Hivites, and the Jebusites, unto a land flowing with milk and honey.

FROM THE BOOK OF EXODUS, CHAPTER 3

THE PASSOVER

This great event in the history of the Jewish people is still celebrated as a reminder of how God saved his people from slavery and gave them freedom. For Christians, it foreshadows the great salvation that Jesus Christ brings to all who trust him.

Moses summoned all the elders of Israel and said, 'Go at once, procure lambs for your families, and slaughter the Passover. Then take a bunch of marjoram, dip it in the blood in the basin, and smear some blood from the basin on the lintel and the two doorposts. Nobody may go out through the door of his house till morning. The Lord will go throughout Egypt and strike it, but when he sees the blood on the lintel and the two doorposts, he will pass over that door and not let the destroyer enter to strike you.

'You are to observe this as a statute for you and your children for all time; when you enter the land which the Lord will give you as he promised, you are to observe this rite. When your children ask you, "What is the meaning of this rite?" you must say, "It is the Lord's Passover, for he passed over the houses of the Israelites in Egypt when he struck the Egyptians and spared our houses."' The people bowed low in worship.

The Israelites went and did exactly as the Lord had commanded Moses and Aaron; and by midnight the Lord had struck down all the firstborn in Egypt, from the firstborn of Pharaoh on his throne to the firstborn of the prisoner in the dungeon, besides the firstborn of cattle. Before night was over Pharaoh rose, he and all his courtiers and all the Egyptians, and there was great wailing, for not a house in Egypt was without its dead. Pharaoh summoned Moses and Aaron while it was still night and said, 'Up with you! Be off, and leave my people, you and the Israelites. Go and worship the Lord, as you request; take your sheep and cattle, and go; and ask God's blessing on me also.'...

At the end of the four hundred and thirty years to the very day, all the tribes of the Lord came out of Egypt. This was the night when the Lord kept vigil to bring them out of Egypt. It is the Lord's night, a vigil for all Israelites generation after generation.

The Lord said to Moses and Aaron: 'This is the statute for the Passover: No foreigner may partake of it; any bought slave may partake provided you have circumcised him; no visitor or hired man may partake of it. Each Passover victim must be eaten inside one house, and you must not take any of the flesh outside. You must not break any of its bones. The whole community of Israel is to keep this feast.

'If aliens settled among you keep the Passover to the Lord, every male among them must first be circumcised, and then he can take part; he will rank as native-born. No male who is uncircumcised may eat of it. The same law will apply both to the native-born and to the alien who is living among you.'

All the Israelites did exactly as the Lord had commanded Moses and Aaron; and on that very day the Lord brought the Israelites out of Egypt mustered in their tribal hosts.

FROM THE BOOK OF EXODUS, CHAPTER 12

37

THE TEN COMMANDMENTS

*A careful reading of God's words, first given to the
people he rescued from slavery in Egypt, shows that
these commandments are more than just a list of rules.
They are concerned with good relationships: the first
four talk about us and God; the last six about how we
treat other people.*

Then God spoke all these words: I am the Lord your God, who
brought you out of the land of Egypt, out of the house of
slavery; you shall have no other gods before me.

You shall not make for yourself an idol, whether in the form of
anything that is in heaven above, or that is on the earth beneath,
or that is in the water under the earth. You shall not bow down to
them or worship them; for I the Lord your God am a jealous God,
punishing children for the iniquity of parents, to the third and the
fourth generation of those who reject me, but showing steadfast
love to the thousandth generation of those who love me and keep
my commandments.

You shall not make wrongful use of the name of the Lord your
God, for the Lord will not acquit anyone who misuses his name.

Remember the sabbath day, and keep it holy.

For six days you shall labour and do all your work. But the
seventh day is a sabbath to the Lord your God; you shall not do
any work – you, your son or your daughter, your male or female
slave, your livestock, or the alien resident in your towns.

For in six days the Lord made heaven and earth, the sea, and
all that is in them, but rested the seventh day; therefore the Lord
blessed the sabbath day and consecrated it.

38

Honour your father and your mother, so that your days may be long in the land that the Lord your God is giving you.

You shall not murder.

You shall not commit adultery.

You shall not steal.

You shall not bear false witness against your neighbour.

You shall not covet your neighbour's house; you shall not covet your neighbour's wife, or male or female slave, or ox, or donkey, or anything that belongs to your neighbour.

FROM THE BOOK OF EXODUS, CHAPTER 20

Joshua's Last Words

*It was Joshua, Moses' successor, who had eventually
taken the Israelites into Canaan, the Promised Land.
His last words remind God's people of God's goodness
to them. Nevertheless, they are not to be forced into
serving God. The choice is theirs.*

And Joshua said unto all the people, Thus saith the Lord God of Israel... I have given you a land for which ye did not labour, and cities which ye built not, and ye dwell in them; of the vineyards and oliveyards which ye planted not do ye eat.

Now therefore fear the Lord, and serve him in sincerity and in truth: and put away the gods which your fathers served on the other side of the flood, and in Egypt; and serve ye the Lord.

And if it seem evil unto you to serve the Lord, choose you this day whom ye will serve; whether the gods which your fathers served that were on the other side of the flood, or the gods of the Amorites, in whose land ye dwell: but as for me and my house, we will serve the Lord...

So Joshua made a covenant with the people that day, and set them a statute and an ordinance in Shechem. And Joshua wrote these words in the book of the law of God, and took a great stone, and set it up there under an oak, that was by the sanctuary of the Lord. And Joshua said unto all the people, Behold, this stone shall be a witness unto us; for it hath heard all the words of the Lord which he spake unto us: it shall be therefore a witness unto you, lest ye deny your God.

FROM THE BOOK OF JOSHUA, CHAPTER 24

SAMSON AND DELILAH

Samson, once God's champion against the Philistine enemy, finds himself conquered in an unexpected way.

And it came to pass afterward, that Samson loved a woman in the valley of Sorek, whose name was Delilah. And the lords of the Philistines came up unto her, and said unto her, Entice him, and see wherein his great strength lieth, and by what means we may prevail against him, that we may bind him to afflict him: and we will give thee every one of us eleven hundred pieces of silver.

And Delilah said to Samson, Tell me, I pray thee, wherein thy great strength lieth, and wherewith thou mightest be bound to afflict thee... And it came to pass, when she pressed him daily with her words, and urged him, so that his soul was vexed unto death; that he told her all his heart, and said unto her, There hath not come a razor upon mine head; for I have been a Nazarite unto God from my mother's womb: if I be shaven, then my strength will go from me, and I shall become weak, and be like any other man.

And when Delilah saw that he had told her all his heart, she sent and called for the lords of the Philistines, saying, Come up this once, for he hath shewed me all his heart. Then the lords of the Philistines came up unto her, and brought money in their hand. And she made him sleep upon her knees; and she called for a man, and she caused him to shave off the seven locks of his head; and she began to afflict him, and his strength went from him.

FROM THE BOOK OF JUDGES, CHAPTER 16

41

THE STORY OF RUTH

This little-known book of the Bible is about family love and a dependence on God. Naomi had come to Moab with her husband and two sons in a time of famine. Now she is a widow living in a foreign land and her sons are dead. Obed, the son of Boaz and Ruth, was the grandfather of David.

Some time later Naomi heard that the Lord had blessed his people by giving them a good harvest; so she got ready to leave Moab with her daughters-in-law.

They started out together to go back to Judah, but on the way she said to them, 'Go back home and stay with your mothers. May the Lord be as good to you as you have been to me and to those who have died. And may the Lord make it possible for each of you to marry again and have a home'...

But Ruth answered, 'Don't ask me to leave you! Let me go with you. Wherever you go, I will go; wherever you live, I will live. Your people will be my people, and your God will be my God. Wherever you die, I will die, and that is where I will be buried. May the Lord's worst punishment come upon me if I let anything but death separate me from you!' When Naomi saw that Ruth was determined to go with her, she said nothing more...

This, then, was how Naomi came back from Moab with Ruth, her Moabite daughter-in-law. The barley harvest was just beginning when they arrived in Bethlehem.

Naomi had a relative named Boaz, a rich and influential man who belonged to the family of her husband Elimelech. One day Ruth said to Naomi, 'Let me go to the fields to gather the corn

42

that the harvest workers leave. I am sure to find someone who will let me work with him.' Naomi answered, 'Go ahead, my daughter.' So Ruth went out to the fields and walked behind the workers, picking up the corn which they left. It so happened that she was in a field that belonged to Boaz.

Some time later Boaz himself arrived from Bethlehem and greeted the workers. 'The Lord be with you!' he said. 'The Lord bless you!' they answered.

Boaz asked the man in charge, 'Who is that young woman?'

The man answered, 'She is the young woman from Moab who came back with Naomi...'

Then Boaz said to Ruth, 'Let me give you some advice. Don't pick up corn anywhere except in this field. Work with the women here; watch them to see where they are reaping and stay with them. I have ordered my men not to molest you. And whenever you are thirsty, go and drink from the water jars that they have filled.'

Ruth bowed down with her face touching the ground, and said to Boaz, 'Why should you be so concerned about me? Why should you be so kind to a foreigner?'

Boaz answered, 'I have heard about everything that you have done for your mother-in-law since your husband died. I know how you left your father and mother and your own country and how you came to live among a people you had never known before. May the Lord reward you for what you have done. May you have a full reward from the Lord God of Israel, to whom you have come for protection!'...

So Boaz took Ruth home as his wife. The Lord blessed her, and she became pregnant and had a son.

FROM THE BOOK OF RUTH, CHAPTERS 1 AND 2

43

THE BOY SAMUEL

Hannah, the mother of Samuel, had been unable to conceive for a number of years. This child was the answer to a desperate prayer, and the fulfilment of a promise: that Hannah's child would serve God in the temple at Shiloh.

In those days, when the boy Samuel was serving the Lord under the direction of Eli, there were very few messages from the Lord, and visions from him were quite rare.

One night Eli, who was now almost blind, was sleeping in his own room; Samuel was sleeping in the sanctuary, where the sacred Covenant Box was. Before dawn, while the lamp was still burning, the Lord called Samuel. He answered, 'Yes, sir!' and ran to Eli and said, 'You called me, and here I am.' But Eli answered, 'I didn't call you; go back to bed.' So Samuel went back to bed.

The Lord called Samuel again. The boy did not know that it was the Lord, because the Lord had never spoken to him before. So he got up, went to Eli, and said, 'You called me, and here I am.' But Eli answered, 'My son, I didn't call you; go back to bed.'

The Lord called Samuel a third time; he got up, went to Eli, and said, 'You called me, and here I am.' Then Eli realized that it was the Lord who was calling the boy, so he said to him, 'Go back to bed; and if he calls you again, say, "Speak, Lord, your servant is listening."' So Samuel went back to bed.

The Lord came and stood there, and called as he had before, 'Samuel! Samuel!' Samuel answered, 'Speak; your servant is listening.'

FROM THE FIRST BOOK OF SAMUEL, CHAPTER 3

44

The Shepherd King

*The prophet Samuel had been given a task: to select
and anoint Israel's next king. His close relationship with
God led him to an unlikely candidate: a young
shepherd-boy called David. David was to become
Israel's greatest king.*

Samuel did what the Lord told him to do and went to
Bethlehem, where the city leaders came trembling to meet
him and asked, 'Is this a peaceful visit, seer?'

'Yes,' he answered. 'I have come to offer a sacrifice to the
Lord. Purify yourselves and come with me.' He also told Jesse
and his sons to purify themselves, and he invited them to the
sacrifice.

When they arrived, Samuel saw Jesse's son Eliab and said to
himself, 'This… is surely the one he has chosen.' But the Lord
said to him, 'Pay no attention to how tall and handsome he is.
I have rejected him, because I do not judge as man judges.
Man looks at the outward appearance, but I look at the heart.'

Then Jesse called his son Abinadab and brought him to
Samuel. But Samuel said, 'No, the Lord hasn't chosen him
either.'

Jesse then brought Shammah. 'No, the Lord hasn't chosen
him either,' Samuel said. In this way Jesse brought seven of his
sons to Samuel. And Samuel said to him, 'No, the Lord hasn't
chosen any of these.' Then he asked him, 'Have you any more
sons?'

Jesse answered, 'There is still the youngest, but he is out
taking care of the sheep.'

45

'Tell him to come here,' Samuel said. 'We won't offer the sacrifice until he comes.' So Jesse sent for him. He was a handsome, healthy young man, and his eyes sparkled.

The Lord said to Samuel, 'This is the one – anoint him!' Samuel took the olive-oil and anointed David in front of his brothers. Immediately the spirit of the Lord took control of David and was with him from that day on. Then Samuel returned to Ramah.

FROM THE FIRST BOOK OF SAMUEL, CHAPTER 16

Solomon's Prayer

Even the fabulous Queen of Sheba came to visit King Solomon, for she had heard of his immense riches, and also of his wisdom. This passage tells us that Solomon's great wisdom was a gift of God from the beginning of his reign.

The king went to Gibeon to sacrifice there, for that was the principal high place; Solomon used to offer a thousand burnt-offerings on that altar. At Gibeon the Lord appeared to Solomon in a dream by night; and God said, 'Ask what I should give you.'

And Solomon said, 'You have shown great and steadfast love to your servant my father David, because he walked before you in faithfulness, in righteousness, and in uprightness of heart towards you; and you have kept for him this great and steadfast love, and have given him a son to sit on his throne today.

'And now, O Lord my God, you have made your servant king in place of my father David, although I am only a little child; I do not know how to go out or come in. And your servant is in the midst of the people whom you have chosen, a great people, so numerous they cannot be numbered or counted. Give your servant therefore an understanding mind to govern your people, able to discern between good and evil; for who can govern this your great people?'

It pleased the Lord that Solomon had asked this. God said to him, 'Because you have asked this, and have not asked for yourself long life or riches, or for the life of your enemies, but

47

have asked for yourself understanding to discern what is right, I now do according to your word. Indeed I give you a wise and discerning mind; no one like you has been before you and no one like you shall arise after you. I give you also what you have not asked, both riches and honour all your life; no other king shall compare with you. If you will walk in my ways, keeping my statutes and my commandments, as your father David walked, then I will lengthen your life.'

Then Solomon awoke; it had been a dream. He came to Jerusalem, where he stood before the ark of the covenant of the Lord. He offered up burnt-offerings and offerings of well-being, and provided a feast for all his servants.

FROM THE FIRST BOOK OF KINGS, CHAPTER 3

JOB

Surely one of the most difficult books of the Bible, the story of Job debates some of life's hardest questions. Why does God allow suffering? What should our response be? This breathtaking passage puts all those questions into an altogether different perspective.

Then out of the storm the Lord spoke to Job. 'Who are you to question my wisdom with your ignorant, empty words? Now stand up straight and answer the questions I ask you.

'Were you there when I made the world? If you know so much, tell me about it. Who decided how large it would be? Who stretched the measuring line over it? Do you know all the answers? What holds up the pillars that support the earth? Who laid the cornerstone of the world? In the dawn of that day the stars sang together, and the heavenly beings shouted for joy.

'Who closed the gates to hold back the sea when it burst from the womb of the earth? It was I who covered the sea with clouds and wrapped it in darkness. I marked a boundary for the sea and kept it behind bolted gates. I told it, "So far and no farther! Here your powerful waves must stop."'

'Job, have you ever in all your life commanded a day to dawn? Have you ordered the dawn to seize the earth and shake the wicked from their hiding places? Daylight makes the hills and valleys stand out like the folds of a garment, clear as the imprint of a seal on clay. The light of day is too bright for the wicked and restrains them from deeds of violence.

'Have you been to the springs in the depths of the sea? Have you walked on the floor of the ocean? Has anyone ever

49

shown you the gates that guard the dark world of the dead? Have you any idea how big the world is? Answer me if you know.'...

Then Job answered the Lord.

'I know, Lord, that you are all-powerful; that you can do everything you want. You ask how I dare question your wisdom when I am so very ignorant. I talked about things I did not understand, about marvels too great for me to know. You told me to listen while you spoke and to try to answer your questions.

'In the past I knew only what others had told me, but now I have seen you with my own eyes. So I am ashamed of all I have said and repent in dust and ashes.'...

Job lived 140 years after this, long enough to see his grandchildren and great-grandchildren. And then he died at a very great age.

FROM THE BOOK OF JOB, CHAPTERS 38 AND 42

50

What is Man?

This psalm, written about 3,000 years ago, is one of the great hymns of worship to God. It would have been sung in King David's time, in Solomon's Temple, in the time of Jesus and is still sung by Christians and Jews throughout the world today.

O Lord our Lord, how excellent is thy name in all the earth! who hast set thy glory above the heavens.

Out of the mouth of babes and sucklings hast thou ordained strength because of thine enemies, that thou mightest still the enemy and the avenger.

When I consider thy heavens, the work of thy fingers, the moon and the stars, which thou hast ordained;

What is man, that thou art mindful of him? and the son of man, that thou visitest him?

For thou hast made him a little lower than the angels, and hast crowned him with glory and honour.

Thou madest him to have dominion over the works of thy hands; thou hast put all things under his feet:

All sheep and oxen, yea, and the beasts of the field; the fowl of the air, and the fish of the sea, and whatsoever passeth through the paths of the seas.

O Lord our Lord, how excellent is thy name in all the earth!

FROM THE BOOK OF PSALMS, CHAPTER 8

THE LORD IS MY SHEPHERD

Psalm 23 is full of tranquil and evocative images. It usually attributed to King David, who as a shepherd-boy must have contemplated the love and care a shepherd has for his sheep as he roamed the hills near Bethlehem. Centuries later, Jesus referred to himself as the 'Good Shepherd'.

The Lord is my shepherd;
   I shall not want.
He maketh me to lie down in green pastures:
   he leadeth me beside the still waters.
He restoreth my soul:
   he leadeth me in the paths of righteousness
   for his name's sake.
Yea, though I walk through the valley
   of the shadow of death, I will fear no evil:
for thou art with me;
   thy rod and thy staff they comfort me.
Thou preparest a table before me
   in the presence of mine enemies:
thou anointest my head with oil;
   my cup runneth over.
Surely goodness and mercy shall follow me
   all the days of my life:
and I will dwell in the house of the Lord
   for ever.

FROM THE BOOK OF PSALMS, CHAPTER 23

In Praise of Wisdom

King Solomon was renowned for his wisdom and is traditionally thought of as the compiler of the book of Proverbs, and writer of a substantial number of them. These wise sayings were intended to help young men live good and righteous lives. Here, 'Wisdom' is personified as a woman.

Does not wisdom call, and does not understanding raise her voice?

On the heights, beside the way, at the crossroads she takes her stand; beside the gates in front of the town, at the entrance of the portals she cries out:

'To you, O people, I call, and my cry is to all that live.

'O simple ones, learn prudence; acquire intelligence, you who lack it.

'Hear, for I will speak noble things, and from my lips will come what is right; for my mouth will utter truth; wickedness is an abomination to my lips.

'All the words of my mouth are righteous; there is nothing twisted or crooked in them.

'They are all straight to one who understands and right to those who find knowledge.

'Take my instruction instead of silver, and knowledge rather than choice gold; for wisdom is better than jewels, and all that you may desire cannot compare with her.

'I, wisdom, live with prudence, and I attain knowledge and discretion... I love those who love me, and those who seek me diligently find me.

53

'Riches and honour are with me, enduring wealth and prosperity.

'My fruit is better than gold, even fine gold, and my yield than choice silver…

'The Lord created me at the beginning of his work, the first of his acts of long ago…

'When he established the heavens, I was there,
when he drew a circle on the face of the deep,
when he made firm the skies above,
when he established the fountains of the deep,
when he assigned to the sea its limit, so that the waters
    might not transgress his command,
when he marked out the foundations of the earth,
    then I was beside him, like a master worker;
and I was daily his delight, rejoicing before him always,
rejoicing in his inhabited world and delighting in the
    human race…

'And now, my children, listen to me: happy are those who keep my ways.

'Hear instruction and be wise, and do not neglect it.

'Happy is the one who listens to me, watching daily at my gates, waiting beside my doors.

'For whoever finds me finds life and obtains favour from the Lord; but those who miss me injure themselves; all who hate me love death.'

FROM THE BOOK OF PROVERBS, CHAPTER 8

A Time for Everything

This famous passage from Ecclesiastes has timeless appeal, and speaks to us today as strongly as it did when it was first written.

For everything there is a season, and a time for every matter under heaven:
 a time to be born, and a time to die;
 a time to plant, and a time to pluck up what is planted;
 a time to kill, and a time to heal;
 a time to break down, and a time to build up;
 a time to weep, and a time to laugh;
 a time to mourn, and a time to dance;
 a time to throw away stones, and a time to gather
  stones together;
 a time to embrace, and a time to refrain from embracing;
 a time to seek, and a time to lose;
 a time to keep, and a time to throw away;
 a time to tear, and a time to sew;
 a time to keep silence, and a time to speak;
 a time to love, and a time to hate;
 a time for war, and a time for peace.

FROM THE BOOK OF ECCLESIASTES, CHAPTER 3

Words of Love

The Song of Solomon is an astonishing collection of love poems. Its sheer exuberance and its erotic nature have drawn forth many different interpretations from scholars over the years. Its place in the Bible confirms God's blessing on the physical expression of love within marriage.

The voice of my beloved! Look, he comes, leaping upon the mountains, bounding over the hills.

My beloved is like a gazelle or a young stag. Look, there he stands behind our wall, gazing in at the windows, looking through the lattice.

My beloved speaks and says to me: 'Arise, my love, my fair one, and come away; for now the winter is past, the rain is over and gone.

'The flowers appear on the earth; the time of singing has come, and the voice of the turtle-dove is heard in our land.

'The fig tree puts forth its figs, and the vines are in blossom; they give forth fragrance. Arise, my love, my fair one, and come away.

'O my dove, in the clefts of the rock, in the covert of the cliff, let me see your face, let me hear your voice; for your voice is sweet, and your face is lovely.'

FROM THE SONG OF SOLOMON, CHAPTER 2

56

Isaiah's Vision

This glorious vision of God was given to the prophet Isaiah in 740BC. God's nation was in religious, moral and political decline. Isaiah catches a vision of God's holiness, and the true sinfulness of humankind.

In the year that King Uzziah died, I saw the Lord sitting on a throne, high and lofty; and the hem of his robe filled the temple. Seraphs were in attendance above him; each had six wings: with two they covered their faces, and with two they covered their feet, and with two they flew. And one called to another and said: 'Holy, holy, holy is the Lord of hosts; the whole earth is full of his glory.' The pivots on the thresholds shook at the voices of those who called, and the house filled with smoke.

And I said: 'Woe is me! I am lost, for I am a man of unclean lips, and I live among a people of unclean lips; yet my eyes have seen the King, the Lord of hosts!'

Then one of the seraphs flew to me, holding a live coal that had been taken from the altar with a pair of tongs. The seraph touched my mouth with it and said: 'Now that this has touched your lips, your guilt has departed and your sin is blotted out.'

Then I heard the voice of the Lord saying, 'Whom shall I send, and who will go for us?' And I said, 'Here am I; send me!'

<small>FROM THE BOOK OF ISAIAH, CHAPTER 6</small>

THE HAND OF THE POTTER

The prophet Jeremiah was frequently the most reviled man in Judah, for in an age when people had turned away from God to worship idols and exploit the poor and weak, he found himself compelled to pass on God's warning. If they did not turn back to God, disaster would overtake them.

The Lord said to me, 'Go down to the potter's house, where I will give you my message.' So I went there and saw the potter working at his wheel. Whenever a piece of pottery turned out imperfect, he would take the clay and make it into something else.

Then the Lord said to me, 'Haven't I the right to do with you people of Israel what the potter did with the clay? You are in my hands just like clay in the potter's hands. If at any time I say that I am going to uproot, break down, or destroy any nation or kingdom, but then that nation turns from its evil, I will not do what I said I would.

'On the other hand, if I say that I am going to plant or build up any nation or kingdom, but then that nation disobeys me and does evil, I will not do what I said I would.

'Now then, tell the people of Judah and of Jerusalem that I am making plans against them and getting ready to punish them. Tell them to stop living sinful lives – to change their ways and the things they are doing. They will answer, "No, why should we? We will all be just as stubborn and evil as we want to be."'

FROM THE BOOK OF JEREMIAH, CHAPTER 18

58

LAMENTATIONS

It is 587BC and Jerusalem has been destroyed by Nebuchadnezzar's army. Most of God's people have been taken away to Babylon; those who remain contemplate the ruins of their once great city and recall the horrors of war. The writer prays to God for forgiveness and restoration.

Remember, O Lord, what has happened to us. Look at us, and see our disgrace. Our property is in the hands of strangers; foreigners are living in our homes. Our fathers have been killed by the enemy, and now our mothers are widows.

We must pay for the water we drink; we must buy the wood we need for fuel. Driven hard like donkeys or camels, we are tired, but are allowed no rest. To get food enough to stay alive, we went begging to Egypt and Assyria.

Our ancestors sinned, but now they are gone, and we are suffering for their sins. We are ruled by those who are no better than slaves, and no one can save us from their power. Murderers roam through the countryside; we risk our lives when we look for food. Hunger has made us burn with fever, until our skin is as hot as an oven.

Our wives have been raped on Mount Zion itself; in every Judean village our daughters have been forced to submit. Our leaders have been taken and hanged; our elders are shown no respect. Our young men are forced to grind corn like slaves; boys go staggering under heavy loads of wood. The old people no longer sit at the city gate, and the young people no longer make music.

Happiness has gone out of our lives; grief has taken the place of our dances. Nothing is left of all we were proud of. We sinned, and now we are doomed. We are sick at our very hearts and can hardly see through our tears, because Mount Zion lies lonely and deserted, and wild jackals prowl through its ruins.

But you, O Lord, are king for ever, and will rule to the end of time. Why have you abandoned us so long? Will you ever remember us again? Bring us back to you, Lord! Bring us back! Restore our ancient glory. Or have you rejected us for ever? Is there no limit to your anger?

FROM THE BOOK OF LAMENTATIONS, CHAPTER 5

DANIEL IN THE LION'S DEN

*Look at this story again through adult eyes. Daniel, an
exile in a foreign land and highly regarded by the king, is
loyal to God. By scheming, his enemies force the king
into a corner. Now it is the king who turns to Daniel's
God; his faith is rewarded. (And the accusers are
thrown to the lions!)*

Now when Daniel knew that the writing was signed, he
went into his house; and his windows being open in his
chamber toward Jerusalem, he kneeled upon his knees three
times a day, and prayed, and gave thanks before his God, as he
did aforetime.

Then these men assembled, and found Daniel praying and
making supplication before his God. Then they came near, and
spake before the king concerning the king's decree; Hast thou
not signed a decree, that every man that shall ask a petition of
any God or man within thirty days, save of thee, O king, shall be
cast into the den of lions? The king answered and said, The
thing is true, according to the law of the Medes and Persians,
which altereth not.

Then answered they and said before the king, That Daniel,
which is of the children of the captivity of Judah, regardeth
not thee, O king, nor the decree that thou hast signed, but
maketh his petition three times a day.

Then the king, when he heard these words, was sore
displeased with himself, and set his heart on Daniel to deliver
him: and he laboured till the going down of the sun to deliver
him.

61

Then these men assembled unto the king, and said unto the king, Know, O king, that the law of the Medes and Persians is, That no decree nor statute which the king establisheth may be changed.

Then the king commanded, and they brought Daniel, and cast him into the den of lions. Now the king spake and said unto Daniel, Thy God whom thou servest continually, he will deliver thee. And a stone was brought, and laid upon the mouth of the den; and the king sealed it with his own signet, and with the signet of his lords; that the purpose might not be changed concerning Daniel.

Then the king went to his palace, and passed the night fasting: neither were instruments of musick brought before him: and his sleep went from him.

Then the king arose very early in the morning, and went in haste unto the den of lions. And when he came to the den, he cried with a lamentable voice unto Daniel: and the king spake and said to Daniel, O Daniel, servant of the living God, is thy God, whom thou servest continually, able to deliver thee from the lions?

Then said Daniel unto the king, O king, live for ever. My God hath sent his angel, and hath shut the lions' mouths, that they have not hurt me: forasmuch as before him innocency was found in me; and also before thee, O king, have I done no hurt.

Then was the king exceeding glad for him, and commanded that they should take Daniel up out of the den. So Daniel was taken up out of the den, and no manner of hurt was found upon him, because he believed in his God. And the king commanded, and they brought those men which had accused Daniel, and they cast them into the den of lions, them, their children, and their wives; and the lions had the mastery of them, and brake all their bones in pieces or ever they came at the bottom of the den.

FROM THE BOOK OF DANIEL, CHAPTER 6

PART TWO

THE NEW TESTAMENT

IN THE BEGINNING

This testimony of John is often read at Christmas, introduced by the words 'St John unfolds the mystery of the incarnation.' It is indeed a mystery that the Creator of the universe, who was there 'in the beginning', should be 'made flesh' and dwell (the Greek can be translated 'pitch his tent') among us.

In the beginning was the Word, and the Word was with God, and the Word was God. The same was in the beginning with God. All things were made by him; and without him was not any thing made that was made. In him was life; and the life was the light of men. And the light shineth in darkness; and the darkness comprehended it not.

There was a man sent from God, whose name was John. The same came for a witness, to bear witness of the Light, that all men through him might believe. He was not that Light, but was sent to bear witness of that Light.

That was the true Light, which lighteth every man that cometh into the world. He was in the world, and the world was made by him, and the world knew him not. He came unto his own, and his own received him not. But as many as received him, to them gave he power to become the sons of God, even to them that believe on his name: which were born, not of blood, nor of the will of the flesh, nor of the will of man, but of God. And the Word was made flesh, and dwelt among us, (and we beheld his glory, the glory as of the only begotten of the Father,) full of grace and truth.

FROM THE GOSPEL OF JOHN, CHAPTER 1

THE BIRTH OF JESUS

*Our familiarity with this story can give us a
distorted view of what Luke wants to tell us. Mary
shows great willingness to obey God, but for the Lord
of the universe to be born in an occupied country in
unsanitary conditions and visited by the lowest members
of society was unexpected, not to say risky!*

And in the sixth month the angel Gabriel was sent from
God unto a city of Galilee, named Nazareth, to a virgin
espoused to a man whose name was Joseph, of the house of
David; and the virgin's name was Mary.

And the angel came in unto her, and said, Hail, thou that
art highly favoured, the Lord is with thee: blessed art thou
among women. And when she saw him, she was troubled at
his saying, and cast in her mind what manner of salutation
this should be.

And the angel said unto her, Fear not, Mary: for thou hast
found favour with God. And, behold, thou shalt conceive in
thy womb, and bring forth a son, and shalt call his name Jesus.
He shall be great, and shall be called the Son of the Highest:
and the Lord God shall give unto him the throne of his father
David: and he shall reign over the house of Jacob for ever;
and of his kingdom there shall be no end.

Then said Mary unto the angel, How shall this be, seeing
I know not a man? And the angel answered and said unto her,
The Holy Ghost shall come upon thee, and the power of the
Highest shall overshadow thee: therefore also that holy thing
which shall be born of thee shall be called the Son of God...

And Mary said, Behold the handmaid of the Lord; be it unto me according to thy word. And the angel departed from her...

And it came to pass in those days, that there went out a decree from Caesar Augustus, that all the world should be taxed. (And this taxing was first made when Cyrenius was governor of Syria.) And all went to be taxed, every one into his own city. And Joseph also went up from Galilee, out of the city of Nazareth, into Judaea, unto the city of David, which is called Bethlehem; (because he was of the house and lineage of David:) to be taxed with Mary his espoused wife, being great with child.

And so it was, that, while they were there, the days were accomplished that she should be delivered. And she brought forth her firstborn son, and wrapped him in swaddling clothes, and laid him in a manger; because there was no room for them in the inn.

And there were in the same country shepherds abiding in the field, keeping watch over their flock by night. And, lo, the angel of the Lord came upon them, and the glory of the Lord shone round about them: and they were sore afraid. And the angel said unto them, Fear not: for, behold, I bring you good tidings of great joy, which shall be to all people. For unto you is born this day in the city of David a Saviour, which is Christ the Lord. And this shall be a sign unto you; Ye shall find the babe wrapped in swaddling clothes, lying in a manger.

And suddenly there was with the angel a multitude of the heavenly host praising God, and saying, Glory to God in the highest, and on earth peace, good will toward men.

And it came to pass, as the angels were gone away from them into heaven, the shepherds said one to another, Let us now go even unto Bethlehem, and see this thing which is come to pass, which the Lord hath made known unto us. And they came with haste, and found Mary, and Joseph, and the babe lying in a manger.

And when they had seen it, they made known abroad the saying which was told them concerning this child. And all they that heard it wondered at those things which were told them by the shepherds.

FROM THE GOSPEL OF LUKE, CHAPTERS 1 AND 2

Jesus Grows Up

This is the only incident mentioned in the gospels concerning Jesus' childhood. At twelve years of age, a Jewish boy received preparation to enter into the adult religious community. By recounting this event, Luke is underlining Jesus' awareness of his relationship with God his Father.

Now it was the practice of Jesus' parents to go to Jerusalem every year for the Passover festival; and when he was twelve, they made the pilgrimage as usual. When the festive season was over and they set off for home, the boy Jesus stayed behind in Jerusalem. His parents did not know of this; but supposing that he was with the party they travelled for a whole day, and only then did they begin looking for him among their friends and relations. When they could not find him they returned to Jerusalem to look for him; and after three days they found him sitting in the temple surrounded by the teachers, listening to them and putting questions; and all who heard him were amazed at his intelligence and the answers he gave. His parents were astonished to see him there, and his mother said to him, 'My son, why have you treated us like this? Your father and I have been anxiously searching for you.' 'Why did you search for me?' he said. 'Did you not know that I was bound to be in my Father's house?' But they did not understand what he meant.

FROM THE GOSPEL OF LUKE, CHAPTER 2

68

JOHN THE BAPTIST

*John, the cousin of Jesus, had a role to fulfil: he was
the herald who announced the coming of the King; the
prophet who opened the way for what God was to do.
His message and his behaviour excited interest and
hostility. His only response was to express his humility.*

The Jewish authorities in Jerusalem sent some priests and
Levites to John, to ask him, 'Who are you?' John did not
refuse to answer, but spoke out openly and clearly, saying:
'I am not the Messiah.'

'Who are you, then?' they asked. 'Are you Elijah?'

'No, I am not,' John answered.

'Are you the Prophet?' they asked. 'No,' he replied.

'Then tell us who you are,' they said. 'We have to take an
answer back to those who sent us. What do you say about
yourself?'

John answered by quoting the prophet Isaiah: 'I am the
voice of someone shouting in the desert: "Make a straight path
for the Lord to travel!"'

The messengers, who had been sent by the Pharisees, then
asked John, 'If you are not the Messiah nor Elijah nor the
Prophet, why do you baptize?'

John answered, 'I baptize with water, but among you stands
the one you do not know. He is coming after me, but I am not
good enough even to untie his sandals.'

All this happened in Bethany on the east side of the River
Jordan, where John was baptizing.

FROM THE GOSPEL OF JOHN, CHAPTER 1

Jesus is Baptized

People were drawn to John the Baptist. The waters of baptism represented their desire to turn away from wrong-doing and start afresh. But surely Jesus did not need to be baptized? However it was a way of identifying with humankind – the sinners he came to save.

Now John wore clothing of camel's hair with a leather belt around his waist, and his food was locusts and wild honey. Then the people of Jerusalem and all Judea were going out to him, and all the region along the Jordan, and they were baptized by him in the river Jordan, confessing their sins...

[John said] 'I baptize you with water for repentance, but one who is more powerful than I is coming after me; I am not worthy to carry his sandals. He will baptize you with the Holy Spirit and fire. His winnowing-fork is in his hand, and he will clear his threshing-floor and will gather his wheat into the granary; but the chaff he will burn with unquenchable fire.'

Then Jesus came from Galilee to John at the Jordan, to be baptized by him. John would have prevented him, saying, 'I need to be baptized by you, and do you come to me?' But Jesus answered him, 'Let it be so now; for it is proper for us in this way to fulfil all righteousness.' Then he consented.

And when Jesus had been baptized, just as he came up from the water, suddenly the heavens were opened to him and he saw the Spirit of God descending like a dove and alighting on him. And a voice from heaven said, 'This is my Son, the Beloved, with whom I am well pleased.'

From the gospel of Matthew, chapter 3

JESUS' TEMPTATION

*'This is my Son, the Beloved.' With the words of his
Father still echoing in his ears, Jesus goes out alone into
the desert to prepare for his ministry. It is a time of
severe testing.*

Then Jesus was led up by the Spirit into the wilderness to
be tempted by the devil. He fasted for forty days and forty
nights, and afterwards he was famished.

The tempter came and said to him, 'If you are the Son of
God, command these stones to become loaves of bread.'

But he answered, 'It is written, "One does not live by bread
alone, but by every word that comes from the mouth of God."'

Then the devil took him to the holy city and placed him on
the pinnacle of the temple, saying to him, 'If you are the Son of
God, throw yourself down; for it is written, "He will command
his angels concerning you", and "On their hands they will bear
you up, so that you will not dash your foot against a stone."'
Jesus said to him, 'Again it is written, "Do not put the Lord
your God to the test."'

Again, the devil took him to a very high mountain and
showed him all the kingdoms of the world and their splendour;
and he said to him, 'All these I will give you, if you will fall
down and worship me.'

Jesus said to him, 'Away with you, Satan! for it is written,
"Worship the Lord your God, and serve only him."'

Then the devil left him, and suddenly angels came and
waited on him.

FROM THE GOSPEL OF MATTHEW, CHAPTER 4

FULFILLED IN JESUS

After Jesus' baptism and temptation in the desert, he returned to Galilee, teaching throughout the region and gathering a great following. In the synagogue in Nazareth, Jesus places his work and his very existence in context.

He [Jesus] came to Nazara, where he had been brought up, and went into the synagogue on the Sabbath day as he usually did. He stood up to read, and they handed him the scroll of the prophet Isaiah. Unrolling the scroll he found the place where it is written:

> The spirit of the Lord is on me,
> for he has anointed me
> to bring the good news to the afflicted.
> He has sent me
>   to proclaim liberty to captives,
> sight to the blind,
> to let the oppressed go free,
> to proclaim a year of favour
>   from the Lord.

He then rolled up the scroll, gave it back to the assistant and sat down. And all eyes in the synagogue were fixed on him. Then he began to speak to them, 'This text is being fulfilled today even while you are listening.'

FROM THE GOSPEL OF LUKE, CHAPTER 4

72

A Wedding at Cana

Jesus' first miracle takes place in the midst of a village wedding. The miracle is not just about alleviating the embarrassment of the bridegroom, whose role it was to provide the wine, but also the first sign of God's transforming power at work in Jesus.

Two days later there was a wedding in the town of Cana in Galilee. Jesus' mother was there, and Jesus and his disciples had also been invited to the wedding. When the wine had given out, Jesus' mother said to him, 'They have no wine left.'

'You must not tell me what to do,' Jesus replied. 'My time has not yet come.' Jesus' mother then told the servants, 'Do whatever he tells you.'

The Jews have rules about ritual washing, and for this purpose six stone water jars were there, each one large enough to hold about a hundred litres. Jesus said to the servants, 'Fill these jars with water. They filled them to the brim, and then he told them, 'Now draw some water out and take it to the man in charge of the feast.' They took him the water, which now had turned into wine, and he tasted it. He did not know where this wine had come from (but, of course, the servants who had drawn out the water knew); so he called the bridegroom and said to him, 'Everyone else serves the best wine first, and after the guests have had plenty to drink, he serves the ordinary wine. But you have kept the best wine until now!'

Jesus performed this first miracle in Cana in Galilee; there he revealed his glory, and his disciples believed in him.

From the gospel of John, chapter 2

BORN OF THE SPIRIT

In this conversation with Nicodemus, Jesus speaks of the new beginning, a re-birth, which he has come to bring. It is not a physical birth, nor is it dependent on wealth, learning or social standing, but it comes from the Spirit, through believing in Jesus, and brings eternal life.

Now there was a Pharisee named Nicodemus, a leader of the Jews. He came to Jesus by night and said to him, 'Rabbi, we know that you are a teacher who has come from God; for no one can do these signs that you do apart from the presence of God.'

Jesus answered him, 'Very truly, I tell you, no one can see the kingdom of God without being born from above.'

Nicodemus said to him, 'How can anyone be born after having grown old? Can one enter a second time into the mother's womb and be born?'

Jesus answered, 'Very truly, I tell you, no one can enter the kingdom of God without being born of water and Spirit. What is born of the flesh is flesh, and what is born of the Spirit is spirit. Do not be astonished that I said to you, "You must be born from above." The wind blows where it chooses, and you hear the sound of it, but you do not know where it comes from or where it goes. So it is with everyone who is born of the Spirit.'

Nicodemus said to him, 'How can these things be?'

Jesus answered him, 'Are you a teacher of Israel, and yet you do not understand these things? Very truly, I tell you, we speak of what we know and testify to what we have seen; yet you do not receive our testimony. If I have told you about earthly things and

74

you do not believe, how can you believe if I tell you about heavenly things? No one has ascended into heaven except the one who descended from heaven, the Son of Man. And just as Moses lifted up the serpent in the wilderness, so must the Son of Man be lifted up, that whoever believes in him may have eternal life. For God so loved the world that he gave his only Son, so that everyone who believes in him may not perish but may have eternal life. Indeed, God did not send the Son into the world to condemn the world, but in order that the world might be saved through him.'

FROM THE GOSPEL OF JOHN, CHAPTER 3

THE SERMON ON THE MOUNT

Sometimes called The Beatitudes, these sayings of Jesus are hard for us to understand. The secret may be in the first line: those who recognize their spiritual poverty and turn to God, find their priorities in life changed, and become more like Jesus.

Blessed are the poor in spirit: for theirs is the kingdom of heaven.

Blessed are they that mourn: for they shall be comforted.

Blessed are the meek: for they shall inherit the earth.

Blessed are they which do hunger and thirst after righteousness: for they shall be filled.

Blessed are the merciful: for they shall obtain mercy.

Blessed are the pure in heart: for they shall see God.

Blessed are the peacemakers: for they shall be called the children of God.

Blessed are they which are persecuted for righteousness' sake: for theirs is the kingdom of heaven.

Blessed are ye, when men shall revile you, and persecute you, and shall say all manner of evil against you falsely, for my sake.

Rejoice, and be exceeding glad: for great is your reward in heaven: for so persecuted they the prophets which were before you.

FROM THE GOSPEL OF MATTHEW, CHAPTER 5

Jesus Stills a Storm

Much of Jesus' time was spent with his disciples on the shores of Lake Galilee. A number of the disciples were experienced sailors, but look at their reactions: even they are amazed as Jesus demonstrates the power of God over nature.

On the evening of that same day Jesus said to his disciples, 'Let us go across to the other side of the lake.' So they left the crowd; the disciples got into the boat in which Jesus was already sitting, and they took him with them. Other boats were there too. Suddenly a strong wind blew up, and the waves began to spill over into the boat, so that it was about to fill with water.

Jesus was in the back of the boat, sleeping with his head on a pillow. The disciples woke him up and said, 'Teacher, don't you care that we are about to die?'

Jesus stood up and commanded the wind, 'Be quiet!' and he said to the waves, 'Be still!' The wind died down, and there was a great calm.

Then Jesus said to his disciples, 'Why are you frightened? Have you still no faith?' But they were terribly afraid and said to one another, 'Who is this man? Even the wind and the waves obey him!'

FROM THE GOSPEL OF MARK, CHAPTER 4

THE LORD'S PRAYER

The Lord's Prayer is surely one of the most well-known prayers of all time. It is simple, yet highly profound, and encourages us to remove the focus from ourselves and to place our trust in God to meet our every need.

Our Father in heaven,
may your name be held holy,
your kingdom come,
your will be done,
on earth as in heaven.
Give us today our daily bread.
And forgive us our debts,
as we have forgiven those
   who are in debt to us.
And do not put us to the test,
but save us from the Evil One.

FROM THE GOSPEL OF MATTHEW, CHAPTER 6

'TALITHA CUMI'

The gospels show Jesus meeting with many different people. Jairus is a respected leader in the community, and he puts his faith in Jesus. His child is dead and the mourning well under way by the time Jesus arrives. In the quietness of her room, Jesus speaks to her.

And when Jesus was passed over again by ship unto the other side, much people gathered unto him: and he was nigh unto the sea. And, behold, there cometh one of the rulers of the synagogue, Jairus by name; and when he saw him, he fell at his feet, And besought him greatly, saying, My little daughter lieth at the point of death: I pray thee, come and lay thy hands on her, that she may be healed; and she shall live.

And Jesus went with him; and much people followed him, and thronged him…

While he yet spake, there came from the ruler of the synagogue's house certain which said, Thy daughter is dead: why troublest thou the Master any further?

As soon as Jesus heard the word that was spoken, he saith unto the ruler of the synagogue, Be not afraid, only believe.

And he suffered no man to follow him, save Peter, and James, and John the brother of James. And he cometh to the house of the ruler of the synagogue, and seeth the tumult, and them that wept and wailed greatly.

And when he was come in, he saith unto them, Why make ye this ado, and weep? the damsel is not dead, but sleepeth.

And they laughed him to scorn. But when he had put them all out, he taketh the father and the mother of the damsel, and them that were with him, and entereth in where the damsel was lying.

And he took the damsel by the hand, and said unto her, Talitha cumi; which is, being interpreted, Damsel, I say unto thee, arise.

And straightway the damsel arose, and walked; for she was of the age of twelve years. And they were astonished with a great astonishment.

And he charged them straitly that no man should know it; and commanded that something should be given her to eat.

FROM THE GOSPEL OF MARK, CHAPTER 5

FOOD FOR
FIVE THOUSAND

Wherever he went, Jesus was followed by crowds of people, eager to hear the good news of the Kingdom of God. Even when he was tired, Jesus was ready to meet their needs, for he said, 'I am the Bread of Life.'

Now the Passover, the festival of the Jews, was near. When he looked up and saw a large crowd coming towards him, Jesus said to Philip, 'Where are we to buy bread for these people to eat?' He said this to test him, for he himself knew what he was going to do. Philip answered him, 'Six months' wages would not buy enough bread for each of them to get a little.'

One of his disciples, Andrew, Simon Peter's brother, said to him, 'There is a boy here who has five barley loaves and two fish. But what are they among so many people?' Jesus said, 'Make the people sit down.' Now there was a great deal of grass in the place; so they sat down, about five thousand in all.

Then Jesus took the loaves, and when he had given thanks, he distributed them to those who were seated; so also the fish, as much as they wanted. When they were satisfied, he told his disciples, 'Gather up the fragments left over, so that nothing may be lost.' So they gathered them up, and from the fragments of the five barley loaves, left by those who had eaten, they filled twelve baskets. When the people saw the sign that he had done, they began to say, 'This is indeed the prophet who is to come into the world.'

FROM THE GOSPEL OF JOHN, CHAPTER 6

81

THE TRANSFIGURATION

Jesus' closest friends, Peter, John and James, never forgot this day. It is thought that this glorious revelation of Jesus as Messiah took place on Mount Hermon. Moses the great Law-giver and Elijah [Elias] the great prophet talk to Jesus of his death, and of what lies ahead.

And it came to pass about an eight days after these sayings, [Jesus] took Peter and John and James, and went up into a mountain to pray. And as he prayed, the fashion of his countenance was altered, and his raiment was white and glistering.

And, behold, there talked with him two men, which were Moses and Elias: who appeared in glory, and spake of his decease which he should accomplish at Jerusalem.

But Peter and they that were with him were heavy with sleep: and when they were awake, they saw his glory, and the two men that stood with him.

And it came to pass, as they departed from him, Peter said unto Jesus, Master, it is good for us to be here: and let us make three tabernacles; one for thee, and one for Moses, and one for Elias: not knowing what he said.

While he thus spake, there came a cloud, and overshadowed them: and they feared as they entered into the cloud. And there came a voice out of the cloud, saying, This is my beloved Son: hear him.

And when the voice was past, Jesus was found alone. And they kept it close, and told no man in those days any of those things which they had seen.

FROM THE GOSPEL OF LUKE, CHAPTER 9

I AM

When God revealed his name to Moses, he said, 'I am who I am.' For the Jews the words 'I am' signified God's name. When Jesus reveals his identity by using this name, he faces the punishment for blasphemy – stoning.

Then answered the Jews, and said unto him, Say we not well that thou art a Samaritan, and hast a devil?

Jesus answered, I have not a devil; but I honour my Father, and ye do dishonour me. And I seek not mine own glory: there is one that seeketh and judgeth. Verily, verily, I say unto you, If a man keep my saying, he shall never see death.

Then said the Jews unto him, Now we know that thou hast a devil. Abraham is dead, and the prophets; and thou sayest, If a man keep my saying, he shall never taste of death. Art thou greater than our father Abraham, which is dead? and the prophets are dead: whom makest thou thyself?

Jesus answered, If I honour myself, my honour is nothing: it is my Father that honoureth me; of whom ye say, that he is your God: Yet ye have not known him; but I know him: and if I should say, I know him not, I shall be a liar like unto you: but I know him, and keep his saying. Your father Abraham rejoiced to see my day: and he saw it, and was glad. Then said the Jews unto him, Thou art not yet fifty years old, and hast thou seen Abraham? Jesus said unto them, Verily, verily, I say unto you, Before Abraham was, I am. Then took they up stones to cast at him: but Jesus hid himself, and went out of the temple, going through the midst of them, and so passed by.

FROM THE GOSPEL OF JOHN, CHAPTER 8

Come Like a Child

How does our world treat children? As unimportant, insignificant beings who have not yet become 'real' people? For Jesus, the 'real' people are those who are ready to be vulnerable, trusting, humble, and willing to come to him in simple faith.

People were bringing little children to [Jesus] in order that he might touch them; and the disciples spoke sternly to them.

But when Jesus saw this, he was indignant and said to them, 'Let the little children come to me; do not stop them; for it is to such as these that the kingdom of God belongs. Truly I tell you, whoever does not receive the kingdom of God as a little child will never enter it.'

And he took them up in his arms, laid his hands on them, and blessed them.

FROM THE GOSPEL OF MARK, CHAPTER 10

THE PARABLE OF THE LOST SHEEP

Jesus often used parables – stories which put across a message – to teach people. This picture of a shepherd searching for the one lost sheep underlines Jesus' concern to seek out those who are far away from him, those 'sinners' frowned upon by others who think of themselves as 'good'.

Now all the tax-collectors and sinners were coming near to listen to him. And the Pharisees and the scribes were grumbling and saying, 'This fellow welcomes sinners and eats with them.'

So he told them this parable:

'Which one of you, having a hundred sheep and losing one of them, does not leave the ninety-nine in the wilderness and go after the one that is lost until he finds it? When he has found it, he lays it on his shoulders and rejoices. And when he comes home, he calls together his friends and neighbours, saying to them, "Rejoice with me, for I have found my sheep that was lost." Just so, I tell you, there will be more joy in heaven over one sinner who repents than over ninety-nine righteous people who need no repentance.'

FROM THE GOSPEL OF LUKE, CHAPTER 15

85

THE PARABLE
OF THE YOUNGER SON

Traditionally known as the parable of the prodigal son, this is also the story of the prodigal's older brother. Jesus shows that the wastrel's repentance provokes a surprising response. The father, like God, rejoices; the older brother, like many religious people of Jesus' day, is angry and resentful.

Jesus went on to say, 'There was once a man who had two sons. The younger one said to him, "Father, give me my share of the property now." So the man divided his property between his two sons.

'After a few days the younger son sold his part of the property and left home with the money. He went to a country far away, where he wasted his money in reckless living.

'He spent everything he had. Then a severe famine spread over that country, and he was left without a thing. So he went to work for one of the citizens of that country, who sent him out to his farm to take care of the pigs. He wished he could fill himself with the bean pods the pigs ate, but no one gave him anything to eat.

'At last he came to his senses and said, "All my father's hired workers have more than they can eat, and here I am about to starve! I will get up and go to my father and say, Father, I have sinned against God and against you. I am no longer fit to be called your son; treat me as one of your hired workers."

'So he got up and started back to his father. He was still a long way from home when his father saw him; his heart was filled with pity, and he ran, threw his arms round his son, and kissed him. "Father" the son said, "I have sinned against God and against you. I am no longer fit to be called your son."

'But the father called his servants. "Hurry!" he said. "Bring the best robe and put it on him. Put a ring on his finger and shoes on his feet. Then go and get the prize calf and kill it, and let us celebrate with a feast! For this son of mine was dead, but now he is alive; he was lost, but now he has been found." And so the feasting began. In the meantime the elder son was out in the field. On his way back, when he came close to the house, he heard the music and dancing. So he called one of the servants and asked him, "What's going on?"

"'Your brother has come back home," the servant answered, "and your father has killed the prize calf, because he got him back safe and sound." The elder brother was so angry that he would not go into the house; so his father came out and begged him to come in. But he answered his father, "Look, all these years I have worked for you like a slave, and I have never disobeyed your orders. What have you given me? Not even a goat for me to have a feast with my friends! But this son of yours wasted all your property on prostitutes, and when he comes back home, you kill the prize calf for him!"

"'My son," the father answered, "you are always here with me, and everything I have is yours. But we had to celebrate and be happy, because your brother was dead, but now he is alive; he was lost, but now he has been found."'

FROM THE GOSPEL OF LUKE, CHAPTER 15

87

THE RESURRECTION AND THE LIFE

Lazarus and his two sisters, Mary and Martha, were some of Jesus' closest friends. And now Lazarus is dead. The words 'Jesus wept' convey such sorrow. As Lazarus is raised from death, Jesus points towards his own resurrection, and his promise of eternal life to all those who believe in him.

As soon as Martha heard that Jesus was on his way, she went to meet him, and left Mary sitting at home.

Martha said to Jesus, 'Lord, if you had been here my brother would not have died. Even now I know that God will grant you whatever you ask of him.' Jesus said, 'Your brother will rise again.'

'I know that he will rise again', said Martha, 'at the resurrection on the last day.' Jesus said, 'I am the resurrection and the life. Whoever has faith in me shall live, even though he dies; and no one who lives and has faith in me shall ever die. Do you believe this?' 'I do, Lord,' she answered; 'I believe that you are the Messiah, the Son of God who was to come into the world.'

So saying she went to call her sister Mary and, taking her aside, she said, 'The Master is here and is asking for you.' As soon as Mary heard this she rose and went to him. Jesus had not yet entered the village, but was still at the place where Martha had met him. When the Jews who were in the house condoling with Mary saw her hurry out, they went after her, assuming that she was going to the tomb to weep there.

Mary came to the place where Jesus was, and as soon as she saw him she fell at his feet and said, 'Lord, if you had been here my brother would not have died.' When Jesus saw her weeping and the Jews who had come with her weeping, he was moved with indignation and deeply distressed. 'Where have you laid him?' he asked. They replied, 'Come and see.' Jesus wept. The Jews said, 'How dearly he must have loved him!' But some of them said, 'Could not this man, who opened the blind man's eyes, have done something to keep Lazarus from dying?'

Jesus, again deeply moved, went to the tomb. It was a cave, with a stone placed against it. Jesus said, 'Take away the stone.' Martha, the dead man's sister, said to him, 'Sir, by now there will be a stench; he has been there four days.' Jesus said, 'Did I not tell you that if you have faith you will see the glory of God?' Then they removed the stone.

Jesus looked upwards and said, 'Father, I thank you for hearing me. I know that you always hear me, but I have spoken for the sake of the people standing round, that they may believe it was you who sent me.'

Then he raised his voice in a great cry: 'Lazarus, come out.' The dead man came out, his hands and feet bound with linen bandages, his face wrapped in a cloth. Jesus said, 'Loose him; let him go.'

FROM THE GOSPEL OF JOHN, CHAPTER 11

JESUS HEALS A BLIND MAN

In the gospels we continually see Jesus showing his love for those on the fringes of society – blind, deaf, sick, outcast, and needy people. Here the crowd try to silence the blind beggar, but he recognizes Jesus' authority to heal him. Jesus' question to him is simple: 'What do you want me to do for you?'

They came to Jericho, and as Jesus was leaving with his disciples and a large crowd, a blind beggar named Bartimaeus son of Timaeus was sitting by the road. When he heard that it was Jesus of Nazareth, he began to shout, 'Jesus! Son of David! Take pity on me!'

Many of the people scolded him and told him to be quiet. But he shouted even more loudly, 'Son of David, take pity on me!' Jesus stopped and said, 'Call him.' So they called the blind man. 'Cheer up!' they said. 'Get up, he is calling you.' He threw off his cloak, jumped up, and came to Jesus.

'What do you want me to do for you?' Jesus asked him. 'Teacher,' the blind man answered, 'I want to see again.'

'Go,' Jesus told him, 'your faith has made you well.' At once he was able to see and followed Jesus on the road.

FROM THE GOSPEL OF MARK, CHAPTER 10

90

KING ON A DONKEY

The events of this day are known to Christians as Palm Sunday. Jerusalem is packed with Jewish people from far and wide, there for the Passover Festival celebrating their liberation from slavery in Egypt nearly 1400 years before. It is significant that Jesus rides a humble donkey, not a war-horse.

Jesus sent two disciples, saying to them, 'Go into the village ahead of you, and immediately you will find a donkey tied, and a colt with her; untie them and bring them to me. If anyone says anything to you, just say this, "The Lord needs them." And he will send them immediately.'

This took place to fulfil what had been spoken through the prophet, saying, 'Tell the daughter of Zion, Look, your king is coming to you, humble, and mounted on a donkey, and on a colt, the foal of a donkey.'

The disciples went and did as Jesus had directed them; they brought the donkey and the colt, and put their cloaks on them, and he sat on them. A very large crowd spread their cloaks on the road, and others cut branches from the trees and spread them on the road. The crowds that went ahead of him and that followed were shouting, 'Hosanna to the Son of David! Blessed is the one who comes in the name of the Lord! Hosanna in the highest heaven!'

When he entered Jerusalem, the whole city was in turmoil, asking, 'Who is this?' The crowds were saying, 'This is the prophet Jesus from Nazareth in Galilee.'

FROM THE GOSPEL OF MATTHEW, CHAPTER 21

91

THE LAST SUPPER

It is evening, and the disciples are meeting in an upstairs room in Jerusalem. Here Jesus speaks some of his most profound words, as he shares a simple meal with his friends. He knows he is about to die; and that he faces death alone. Nevertheless, he promises to meet them in Galilee after his death.

And as they were eating, Jesus took bread, and blessed it, and brake it, and gave it to the disciples, and said, Take, eat; this is my body.

And he took the cup, and gave thanks, and gave it to them, saying, Drink ye all of it; For this is my blood of the new testament, which is shed for many for the remission of sins. But I say unto you, I will not drink henceforth of this fruit of the vine, until that day when I drink it new with you in my Father's kingdom.

And when they had sung an hymn, they went out into the mount of Olives. Then saith Jesus unto them, All ye shall be offended because of me this night: for it is written, I will smite the shepherd, and the sheep of the flock shall be scattered abroad. But after I am risen again, I will go before you into Galilee.

Peter answered and said unto him, Though all men shall be offended because of thee, yet will I never be offended.

Jesus said unto him, Verily I say unto thee, That this night, before the cock crow, thou shalt deny me thrice.

Peter said unto him, Though I should die with thee, yet will I not deny thee. Likewise also said all the disciples.

FROM THE GOSPEL OF MATTHEW, CHAPTER 26

Betrayal at Gethsemane

It is night-time in the olive groves of Gethsemane, just outside Jerusalem. Gethsemane is a place that Jesus often visits with his disciples. But this night it is different. Jesus, in agony, faces his death. He prays to his Father, pleading with him. Another gospel writer records that his sweat fell like great drops of blood.

Then Jesus went with them to a place called Gethsemane; and he said to his disciples, 'Sit here while I go over there and pray.' He took with him Peter and the two sons of Zebedee, and began to be grieved and agitated.

Then he said to them, 'I am deeply grieved, even to death; remain here, and stay awake with me.'

And going a little farther, he threw himself on the ground and prayed, 'My Father, if it is possible, let this cup pass from me; yet not what I want but what you want.'

Then he came to the disciples and found them sleeping; and he said to Peter, 'So, could you not stay awake with me one hour? Stay awake and pray that you may not come into the time of trial; the spirit indeed is willing, but the flesh is weak.'

Again he went away for the second time and prayed, 'My Father, if this cannot pass unless I drink it, your will be done.'

Again he came and found them sleeping, for their eyes were heavy. So leaving them again, he went away and prayed for the third time, saying the same words.

Then he came to the disciples and said to them, 'Are you still sleeping and taking your rest? See, the hour is at hand, and the Son of Man is betrayed into the hands of sinners. Get up, let us be going. See, my betrayer is at hand.'

While he was still speaking, Judas, one of the twelve, arrived; with him was a large crowd with swords and clubs, from the chief priests and the elders of the people. Now the betrayer had given them a sign, saying, 'The one I will kiss is the man; arrest him.'

At once he came up to Jesus and said, 'Greetings, Rabbi!' and kissed him. Jesus said to him, 'Friend, do what you are here to do.' Then they came and laid hands on Jesus and arrested him.

Suddenly, one of those with Jesus put his hand on his sword, drew it, and struck the slave of the high priest, cutting off his ear. Then Jesus said to him, 'Put your sword back into its place; for all who take the sword will perish by the sword. Do you think that I cannot appeal to my Father, and he will at once send me more than twelve legions of angels? But how then would the scriptures be fulfilled, which say it must happen in this way?'

At that hour Jesus said to the crowds, 'Have you come out with swords and clubs to arrest me as though I were a bandit? Day after day I sat in the temple teaching, and you did not arrest me. But all this has taken place, so that the scriptures of the prophets may be fulfilled.' Then all the disciples deserted him and fled.

FROM THE GOSPEL OF MATTHEW, CHAPTER 26

JESUS ON TRIAL

The trial before the Jewish Council has finished; they want to put Jesus to death, but the death sentence can only be passed by Roman law. The Roman governor, Pilate, is weak. His popularity with the mob seems more important to him than administering justice.

And straightway in the morning the chief priests held a consultation with the elders and scribes and the whole council, and bound Jesus, and carried him away, and delivered him to Pilate. And Pilate asked him, Art thou the King of the Jews? And he answering said unto him, Thou sayest it.

And the chief priests accused him of many things: but he answered nothing. And Pilate asked him again, saying, Answerest thou nothing? behold how many things they witness against thee. But Jesus yet answered nothing; so that Pilate marvelled.

Now at that feast he released unto them one prisoner, whomsoever they desired. And there was one named Barabbas, which lay bound with them that had made insurrection with him, who had committed murder in the insurrection. And the multitude crying aloud began to desire him to do as he had ever done unto them.

But Pilate answered them, saying, Will ye that I release unto you the King of the Jews? For he knew that the chief priests had delivered him for envy. But the chief priests moved the people, that he should rather release Barabbas unto them. And Pilate answered and said again unto them, What will ye then that I shall do unto him whom ye call the King of the Jews?

And they cried out again, Crucify him.

Then Pilate said unto them, Why, what evil hath he done? And they cried out the more exceedingly, Crucify him.

And so Pilate, willing to content the people, released Barabbas unto them, and delivered Jesus, when he had scourged him, to be crucified.

And the soldiers led him away into the hall, called Praetorium; and they call together the whole band. And they clothed him with purple, and platted a crown of thorns, and put it about his head, and began to salute him, Hail, King of the Jews! And they smote him on the head with a reed, and did spit upon him, and bowing their knees worshipped him.

And when they had mocked him, they took off the purple from him, and put his own clothes on him, and led him out to crucify him.

FROM THE GOSPEL OF MARK, CHAPTER 15

THE CRUCIFIXION

The Romans used crucifixion as a method of execution for slaves, criminals and those who were not Roman citizens. The condemned man was whipped, then had to carry the cross bar to the place of execution. He was nailed to the cross and left to die, a slow, painful, lingering death.

Then Pilate's soldiers took Jesus into the governor's palace, and the whole company gathered round him. They stripped off his clothes and put a scarlet robe on him. Then they made a crown out of thorny branches and placed it on his head, and put a stick in his right hand; then they knelt before him and mocked him. 'Long live the King of the Jews!' they said. They spat on him, and took the stick and hit him over the head.

When they had finished mocking him, they took the robe off and put his own clothes back on him. Then they led him out to crucify him. As they were going out, they met a man from Cyrene named Simon, and the soldiers forced him to carry Jesus' cross.

They came to a place called Golgotha, which means, 'The Place of the Skull'. There they offered Jesus wine mixed with a bitter substance; but after tasting it, he would not drink it. They crucified him and then divided his clothes among them by throwing dice. After that they sat there and watched him. Above his head they put the written notice of the accusation against him: 'This is Jesus, the King of the Jews.' Then they crucified two bandits with Jesus, one on his right and the other on his left.

People passing by shook their heads and hurled insults at Jesus: 'You were going to tear down the Temple and build it up again in three days! Save yourself if you are God's Son! Come on down from the cross!' In the same way the chief priests and the teachers of the Law and the elders jeered at him: 'He saved others, but he cannot save himself! Isn't he the king of Israel? If he comes down off the cross now, we will believe in him! He trusts in God and claims to be God's Son. Well, then, let us see if God wants to save him now!' Even the bandits who had been crucified with him insulted him in the same way.

At noon the whole country was covered with darkness, which lasted for three hours. At about three o'clock Jesus cried out with a loud shout, 'Eli, Eli, lema sabachthani?' which means, 'My God, my God, why did you abandon me?' Some of the people standing there heard him and said, 'He is calling for Elijah!'

One of them ran up at once, took a sponge, soaked it in cheap wine, put it on the end of a stick, and tried to make him drink it. But the others said, 'Wait, let us see if Elijah is coming to save him!'

Jesus again gave a loud cry and breathed his last. Then the curtain hanging in the Temple was torn in two from top to bottom. The earth shook, the rocks split apart, the graves broke open, and many of God's people who had died were raised to life. They left the graves, and after Jesus rose from death, they went into the Holy City, where many people saw them.

When the army officer and the soldiers with him who were watching Jesus saw the earthquake and everything else that happened, they were terrified and said, 'He really was the Son of God!'

FROM THE GOSPEL OF MATTHEW, CHAPTER 27

JESUS IS RISEN

The burial of Jesus had been hasty, the body wrapped in linen clothes and laid in a tomb, hewn out of the rock, before the Sabbath started. The entrance had been sealed with a huge stone. Yet on the third day, he was no longer there. Death could not hold him.

After the Sabbath was over, Mary Magdalene, Mary the mother of James, and Salome bought spices to go and anoint the body of Jesus. Very early on Sunday morning, at sunrise, they went to the tomb. On the way they said to one another, 'Who will roll away the stone for us from the entrance to the tomb?' (It was a very large stone.) Then they looked up and saw that the stone had already been rolled back. So they entered the tomb, where they saw a young man sitting on the right, wearing a white robe – and they were alarmed.

'Don't be alarmed,' he said. 'I know you are looking for Jesus of Nazareth, who was crucified. He is not here – he has been raised! Look, here is the place where they put him. Now go and give this message to his disciples, including Peter: "He is going to Galilee ahead of you; there you will see him, just as he told you." ' So they went out and ran from the tomb, distressed and terrified. They said nothing to anyone, because they were afraid.

FROM THE GOSPEL OF MARK, CHAPTER 16

99

THE WALK TO EMMAUS

This account has an almost dreamlike quality. It is the day after the Sabbath and Jesus has risen. Cleopas and his friend, like the other disciples, are confused and sad. Yet by the end of their journey to Emmaus, their eyes have been opened.

Now on that same day two of them were going to a village called Emmaus, about seven miles from Jerusalem, and talking with each other about all these things that had happened. While they were talking and discussing, Jesus himself came near and went with them, but their eyes were kept from recognizing him.

And he said to them, 'What are you discussing with each other while you walk along?' They stood still, looking sad.

Then one of them, whose name was Cleopas, answered him, 'Are you the only stranger in Jerusalem who does not know the things that have taken place there in these days?'

He asked them, 'What things?' They replied, 'The things about Jesus of Nazareth, who was a prophet mighty in deed and word before God and all the people, and how our chief priests and leaders handed him over to be condemned to death and crucified him. But we had hoped that he was the one to redeem Israel. Yes, and besides all this, it is now the third day since these things took place.

'Moreover, some women of our group astounded us. They were at the tomb early this morning, and when they did not find his body there, they came back and told us that they had indeed seen a vision of angels who said that he was alive.

'Some of those who were with us went to the tomb and found it just as the women had said; but they did not see him.'

Then he said to them, 'Oh, how foolish you are, and how slow of heart to believe all that the prophets have declared! Was it not necessary that the Messiah should suffer these things and then enter into his glory?'

Then beginning with Moses and all the prophets, he interpreted to them the things about himself in all the scriptures.

As they came near the village to which they were going, he walked ahead as if he were going on. But they urged him strongly, saying, 'Stay with us, because it is almost evening and the day is now nearly over.' So he went in to stay with them.

When he was at the table with them, he took bread, blessed and broke it, and gave it to them. Then their eyes were opened, and they recognized him; and he vanished from their sight.

They said to each other, 'Were not our hearts burning within us while he was talking to us on the road, while he was opening the scriptures to us?'

FROM THE GOSPEL OF LUKE, CHAPTER 24

JESUS APPEARS IN GALILEE

Who knows why Simon Peter and his friends went fishing in the days following Jesus' death and resurrection? Fishing had once been their livelihood. Now their empty nets are depressing. Did Jesus come to them just then to remind them that without him their work would be fruitless?

Gathered there together were Simon Peter, Thomas called the Twin, Nathanael of Cana in Galilee, the sons of Zebedee, and two others of his disciples. Simon Peter said to them, 'I am going fishing.' They said to him, 'We will go with you.' They went out and got into the boat, but that night they caught nothing.

Just after daybreak, Jesus stood on the beach; but the disciples did not know that it was Jesus. Jesus said to them, 'Children, you have no fish, have you?'

They answered him, 'No.' He said to them, 'Cast the net to the right side of the boat, and you will find some.' So they cast it, and now they were not able to haul it in because there were so many fish.

That disciple whom Jesus loved said to Peter, 'It is the Lord!' When Simon Peter heard that it was the Lord, he put on some clothes, for he was naked, and jumped into the lake. But the other disciples came in the boat, dragging the net full of fish, for they were not far from the land, only about a hundred yards off. When they had gone ashore, they saw a charcoal fire there, with fish on it, and bread.

Jesus said to them, 'Bring some of the fish that you have just caught.' So Simon Peter went aboard and hauled the net ashore, full of large fish, a hundred and fifty-three of them; and though there were so many, the net was not torn.

Jesus said to them, 'Come and have breakfast.' Now none of the disciples dared to ask him, 'Who are you?' because they knew it was the Lord. Jesus came and took the bread and gave it to them, and did the same with the fish.

This was now the third time that Jesus appeared to the disciples after he was raised from the dead.

FROM THE GOSPEL OF JOHN, CHAPTER 21

THE ASCENSION

*The gospel accounts of Jesus' appearances after his
resurrection stretch our understanding. He can appear
suddenly, but he is not a ghost. He promises 'power' –
the Spirit – to carry on his work and, forty days after
his resurrection, he returns to his Father in heaven.*

While the two were telling them this, suddenly the Lord
himself stood among them and said to them, 'Peace be with
you.' They were terrified, thinking that they were seeing a ghost.
But he said to them, 'Why are you alarmed? Why are these doubts
coming up in your minds? Look at my hands and my feet, and see
that it is I myself. Feel me, and you will know, for a ghost doesn't
have flesh and bones, as you can see I have.'

He said this and showed them his hands and his feet. They still
could not believe, they were so full of joy and wonder; so he asked
them, 'Have you anything here to eat?' They gave him a piece of
cooked fish, which he took and ate in their presence. Then he said
to them, 'These are the very things I told you about while I was
still with you: everything written about me in the Law of Moses,
the writings of the prophets, and the Psalms had to come true.'

Then he opened their minds to understand the Scriptures, and
said to them, 'This is what is written: the Messiah must suffer and
must rise from death three days later, and in his name the message
about repentance and the forgiveness of sins must be preached to
all nations, beginning in Jerusalem. You are witnesses of these
things. And I myself will send upon you what my Father has
promised. But you must wait in the city until the power from
above comes down upon you.'

Then he led them out of the city as far as Bethany, where he raised his hands and blessed them. As he was blessing them, he departed from them and was taken up into heaven.

They worshipped him and went back into Jerusalem, filled with great joy, and spent all their time in the Temple giving thanks to God.

FROM THE GOSPEL OF LUKE, CHAPTER 34

The Day of Pentecost

*Sometimes called 'the birthday of the Church', this is
how the power of the Holy Spirit spread the 'good news'
of Jesus among the Jews first, and later to the rest of the
world (Gentiles), as Jesus had promised.*

And when the day of Pentecost was fully come, they were all
with one accord in one place. And suddenly there came a
sound from heaven as of a rushing mighty wind, and it filled all the
house where they were sitting. And there appeared unto them
cloven tongues like as of fire, and it sat upon each of them. And
they were all filled with the Holy Ghost, and began to speak with
other tongues, as the Spirit gave them utterance.

And there were dwelling at Jerusalem Jews, devout men, out of
every nation under heaven. Now when this was noised abroad, the
multitude came together, and were confounded, because that every
man heard them speak in his own language.

And they were all amazed and marvelled, saying one to another,
Behold, are not all these which speak Galilaeans? And how hear we
every man in our own tongue, wherein we were born? Parthians,
and Medes, and Elamites, and the dwellers in Mesopotamia, and in
Judaea, and Cappadocia, in Pontus, and Asia, Phrygia, and
Pamphylia, in Egypt, and in the parts of Libya about Cyrene, and
strangers of Rome, Jews and proselytes, Cretes and Arabians, we do
hear them speak in our tongues the wonderful works of God.

And they were all amazed, and were in doubt, saying one to
another, What meaneth this?

Others mocking said, These men are full of new wine. But
Peter, standing up with the eleven, lifted up his voice, and said

unto them, Ye men of Judaea, and all ye that dwell at
Jerusalem, be this known unto you, and hearken to my words:
For these are not drunken, as ye suppose, seeing it is but the
third hour of the day. But this is that which was spoken by the
prophet Joel;

And it shall come to pass in the last days, saith God, I will
pour out of my Spirit upon all flesh: and your sons and your
daughters shall prophesy, and your young men shall see visions,
and your old men shall dream dreams:

And on my servants and on my handmaidens I will pour
out in those days of my Spirit; and they shall prophesy:

And I will shew wonders in heaven above, and signs in the
earth beneath; blood, and fire, and vapour of smoke:

The sun shall be turned into darkness, and the moon into
blood, before that great and notable day of the Lord come:

And it shall come to pass, that whosoever shall call on the
name of the Lord shall be saved.

Ye men of Israel, hear these words; Jesus of Nazareth, a
man approved of God among you by miracles and wonders and
signs, which God did by him in the midst of you, as ye
yourselves also know: Him, being delivered by the determinate
counsel and foreknowledge of God, ye have taken, and by
wicked hands have crucified and slain: Whom God hath raised
up, having loosed the pains of death: because it was not
possible that he should be holden of it.

FROM THE BOOK OF ACTS, CHAPTER 2

107

THE ROAD TO DAMASCUS

Saul, an educated man, a good and upright religious person, and a Roman citizen, was dedicated to the persecution of Christians. But his meeting with the risen Lord Jesus changed his life for ever, and had a profound effect on the spread of Christian belief throughout the Roman empire. He is renamed Paul, the apostle.

Saul, still breathing threats and murder against the disciples of the Lord, went to the high priest and asked him for letters to the synagogues at Damascus, so that if he found any who belonged to the Way, men or women, he might bring them bound to Jerusalem.

Now as he was going along and approaching Damascus, suddenly a light from heaven flashed around him. He fell to the ground and heard a voice saying to him, 'Saul, Saul, why do you persecute me?'

He asked, 'Who are you, Lord?'

The reply came, 'I am Jesus, whom you are persecuting. But get up and enter the city, and you will be told what you are to do.' The men who were travelling with him stood speechless because they heard the voice but saw no one.

Saul got up from the ground, and though his eyes were open, he could see nothing; so they led him by the hand and brought him into Damascus. For three days he was without sight, and neither ate nor drank.

Now there was a disciple in Damascus named Ananias. The Lord said to him in a vision, 'Ananias.' He answered, 'Here I am, Lord.'

The Lord said to him, 'Get up and go to the street called Straight, and at the house of Judas look for a man of Tarsus named Saul. At this moment he is praying, and he has seen in a vision a man named Ananias come in and lay his hands on him so that he might regain his sight.'

But Ananias answered, 'Lord, I have heard from many about this man, how much evil he has done to your saints in Jerusalem; and here he has authority from the chief priests to bind all who invoke your name.'

But the Lord said to him, 'Go, for he is an instrument whom I have chosen to bring my name before Gentiles and kings and before the people of Israel; I myself will show him how much he must suffer for the sake of my name.'

So Ananias went and entered the house. He laid his hands on Saul and said, 'Brother Saul, the Lord Jesus, who appeared to you on your way here, has sent me so that you may regain your sight and be filled with the Holy Spirit.'

And immediately something like scales fell from his eyes, and his sight was restored. Then he got up and was baptized, and after taking some food, he regained his strength.

FROM THE BOOK OF ACTS, CHAPTER 9

109

JUSTIFICATION BY FAITH

*Paul was one of the most influential leaders and
teachers in the early Church. Some of his many letters
form part of the New Testament. Here in his letter to
the Christians in Rome, Paul marvels at the freedom
of sins forgiven and Christ's reconciling love.*

Therefore, since we are justified by faith, we have peace with
God through our Lord Jesus Christ, through whom we have
obtained access to this grace in which we stand; and we boast in
our hope of sharing the glory of God.

And not only that, but we also boast in our sufferings, knowing
that suffering produces endurance, and endurance produces
character, and character produces hope, and hope does not
disappoint us, because God's love has been poured into our hearts
through the Holy Spirit that has been given to us.

For while we were still weak, at the right time Christ died for
the ungodly. Indeed, rarely will anyone die for a righteous person –
though perhaps for a good person someone might actually dare to
die. But God proves his love for us in that while we still were
sinners Christ died for us. Much more surely then, now that we
have been justified by his blood, will we be saved through him
from the wrath of God. For if while we were enemies, we were
reconciled to God through the death of his Son, much more surely,
having been reconciled, will we be saved by his life. But more than
that, we even boast in God through our Lord Jesus Christ, through
whom we have now received reconciliation.

Therefore, just as sin came into the world through one man,
and death came through sin, and so death spread to all because all

have sinned – sin was indeed in the world before the law, but sin is not reckoned when there is no law. Yet death exercised dominion from Adam to Moses, even over those whose sins were not like the transgression of Adam, who is a type of the one who was to come.

But the free gift is not like the trespass. For if the many died through the one man's trespass, much more surely have the grace of God and the free gift in the grace of the one man, Jesus Christ, abounded for the many. And the free gift is not like the effect of the one man's sin. For the judgement following one trespass brought condemnation, but the free gift following many trespasses brings justification.

If, because of the one man's trespass, death exercised dominion through that one, much more surely will those who receive the abundance of grace and the free gift of righteousness exercise dominion in life through the one man, Jesus Christ.

Therefore just as one man's trespass led to condemnation for all, so one man's act of righteousness leads to justification and life for all. For just as by the one man's disobedience the many were made sinners, so by the one man's obedience the many will be made righteous.

But law came in, with the result that the trespass multiplied; but where sin increased, grace abounded all the more, so that, just as sin exercised dominion in death, so grace might also exercise dominion through justification leading to eternal life through Jesus Christ our Lord.

FROM THE LETTER TO THE ROMANS, CHAPTER 5

111

BE NOT CONFORMED

Parts of Paul's letters address the practical implications of following Christ. He tells the Roman Christians that they should be different, not 'conformed' to the world, but 'transformed' in body, mind and spirit. As a result, their actions and attitudes will speak of good, and not of evil.

I beseech you therefore, brethren, by the mercies of God, that ye present your bodies a living sacrifice, holy, acceptable unto God, which is your reasonable service. And be not conformed to this world, but be ye transformed by the renewing of your mind, that ye may prove what is that good, and acceptable, and perfect, will of God...

Let love be without dissimulation. Abhor that which is evil; cleave to that which is good. Be kindly affectioned one to another with brotherly love; in honour preferring one another; not slothful in business; fervent in spirit; serving the Lord; rejoicing in hope; patient in tribulation; continuing instant in prayer; distributing to the necessity of saints; given to hospitality.

Bless them which persecute you: bless, and curse not. Rejoice with them that do rejoice, and weep with them that weep. Be of the same mind one toward another. Mind not high things, but condescend to men of low estate. Be not wise in your own conceits. Recompense to no man evil for evil. Provide things honest in the sight of all men. If it be possible, as much as lieth in you, live peaceably with all men.

Dearly beloved, avenge not yourselves, but rather give place unto wrath: for it is written, Vengeance is mine; I will repay, saith the Lord. Therefore if thine enemy hunger, feed him; if he thirst, give him drink: for in so doing thou shalt heap coals of fire on his head. Be not overcome of evil, but overcome evil with good.

FROM THE LETTER TO THE ROMANS, CHAPTER 12

LOVE IS THE GREATEST

This is one of the most dearly loved passages from the Bible. Paul's transcendent prose is in fact part of a rebuke to the church at Corinth whose members had been behaving in less than loving ways.

I may be able to speak the languages of human beings and even of angels, but if I have no love, my speech is no more than a noisy gong or a clanging bell.

I may have the gift of inspired preaching; I may have all knowledge and understand all secrets; I may have all the faith needed to move mountains – but if I have no love, I am nothing.

I may give away everything I have, and even give up my body to be burnt – but if I have no love, this does me no good.

Love is patient and kind; it is not jealous or conceited or proud; love is not ill-mannered or selfish or irritable; love does not keep a record of wrongs; love is not happy with evil, but is happy with the truth. Love never gives up; and its faith, hope, and patience never fail.

Love is eternal. There are inspired messages, but they are temporary; there are gifts of speaking in strange tongues, but they will cease; there is knowledge, but it will pass. For our gifts of knowledge and of inspired messages are only partial; but when what is perfect comes, then what is partial will disappear…

What I know now is only partial; then it will be complete – as complete as God's knowledge of me. Meanwhile these three remain: faith, hope, and love; and the greatest of these is love.

FROM THE FIRST LETTER TO THE CORINTHIANS, CHAPTER 13

THE STING OF DEATH

Greeks believed in the immortality of the soul, but not in the resurrection of the body. Earlier in this chapter, Paul reminded his readers that Christ's resurrection is at the heart of faith, and, twenty-five years after the event, there are still witnesses to prove it. But what is the nature of the resurrection body?

But someone will ask, 'How are the dead raised? With what kind of body do they come?'

Fool! What you sow does not come to life unless it dies. And as for what you sow, you do not sow the body that is to be, but a bare seed, perhaps of wheat or of some other grain. But God gives it a body as he has chosen, and to each kind of seed its own body.

Not all flesh is alike, but there is one flesh for human beings, another for animals, another for birds, and another for fish. There are both heavenly bodies and earthly bodies, but the glory of the heavenly is one thing, and that of the earthly is another. There is one glory of the sun, and another glory of the moon, and another glory of the stars; indeed, star differs from star in glory.

So it is with the resurrection of the dead. What is sown is perishable, what is raised is imperishable. It is sown in dishonour, it is raised in glory. It is sown in weakness, it is raised in power. It is sown a physical body, it is raised a spiritual body. If there is a physical body, there is also a spiritual body...

Listen, I will tell you a mystery! We will not all die, but we will all be changed, in a moment, in the twinkling of an eye, at the last trumpet. For the trumpet will sound, and the dead will be raised imperishable, and we will be changed.

For this perishable body must put on imperishability, and this mortal body must put on immortality.

When this perishable body puts on imperishability, and this mortal body puts on immortality, then the saying that is written will be fulfilled: 'Death has been swallowed up in victory.'

'Where, O death, is your victory? Where, O death, is your sting?' The sting of death is sin, and the power of sin is the law. But thanks be to God, who gives us the victory through our Lord Jesus Christ.

FROM THE FIRST LETTER TO THE CORINTHIANS, CHAPTER 15

The Armour of God

Paul, writing to the Christians at Ephesus, starts his letter by exploring what the new life 'in Christ' means. He then moves on to the practical questions of how this affects human relationships. This last passage puts forward a more 'cosmic' view of life as a Christian: there is a battle to be fought, but the armour is provided.

Finally, be strong in the Lord and in the strength of his power. Put on the whole armour of God, so that you may be able to stand against the wiles of the devil.

For our struggle is not against enemies of blood and flesh, but against the rulers, against the authorities, against the cosmic powers of this present darkness, against the spiritual forces of evil in the heavenly places. Therefore take up the whole armour of God, so that you may be able to withstand on that evil day, and having done everything, to stand firm.

Stand therefore, and fasten the belt of truth around your waist, and put on the breastplate of righteousness. As shoes for your feet put on whatever will make you ready to proclaim the gospel of peace. With all of these, take the shield of faith, with which you will be able to quench all the flaming arrows of the evil one. Take the helmet of salvation, and the sword of the Spirit, which is the word of God.

Pray in the Spirit at all times in every prayer and supplication. To that end keep alert and always persevere in supplication for all the saints. Pray also for me, so that when I speak, a message may be given to me to make known with boldness the mystery of the gospel, for which I am an ambassador in chains. Pray that I may declare it boldly, as I must speak.

FROM THE LETTER TO THE EPHESIANS, CHAPTER 6

THE PEACE OF GOD

If God is the provider of strength, he is also the bringer of peace. It is likely that Paul wrote to the church at Philippi while he was imprisoned in Rome, and yet his letter is one of thankfulness and even joy, as he trusts and rests in God's peace. Here, he calls the Philippians to do likewise.

Rejoice in the Lord always. I will say it again: Rejoice! Let your gentleness be evident to all. The Lord is near. Do not be anxious about anything, but in everything, by prayer and petition, with thanksgiving, present your requests to God. And the peace of God, which transcends all understanding, will guard your hearts and your minds in Christ Jesus.

Finally, brothers, whatever is true, whatever is noble, whatever is right, whatever is pure, whatever is lovely, whatever is admirable – think about such things. Whatever you have learned or received or heard from me, or seen in me – put it into practice. And the God of peace will be with you.

FROM THE LETTER TO THE PHILIPPIANS, CHAPTER 4

FIGHT THE GOOD FIGHT

Timothy was a young Christian leader who had accompanied Paul on many of his travels. The New Testament contains two letters from Paul addressed to Timothy. In this passage Paul exhorts Timothy to 'flee' from false doctrines and the pursuit of riches, and to persevere in the faith.

But thou, O man of God, flee these things; and follow after righteousness, godliness, faith, love, patience, meekness. Fight the good fight of faith, lay hold on eternal life, whereunto thou art also called, and hast professed a good profession before many witnesses.

I give thee charge in the sight of God, who quickeneth all things, and before Christ Jesus, who before Pontius Pilate witnessed a good confession; that thou keep this commandment without spot, unrebukeable, until the appearing of our Lord Jesus Christ: which in his times he shall shew, who is the blessed and only Potentate, the King of kings, and Lord of lords; who only hath immortality, dwelling in the light which no man can approach unto; whom no man hath seen, nor can see: to whom be honour and power everlasting. Amen.

FROM THE FIRST LETTER TO TIMOTHY, CHAPTER 6

120

THE TONGUE IS A FIRE

All of us have at some time said something we have immediately regretted. Here, James' letter looks at the power of words.

All of us often make mistakes. But if a person never makes a mistake in what he says, he is perfect and is also able to control his whole being. We put a bit into the mouth of a horse to make it obey us, and we are able to make it go where we want. Or think of a ship: big as it is and driven by such strong winds, it can be steered by a very small rudder, and it goes wherever the pilot wants it to go.

So it is with the tongue: small as it is, it can boast about great things. Just think how large a forest can be set on fire by a tiny flame! And the tongue is like a fire. It is a world of wrong, occupying its place in our bodies and spreading evil through our whole being. It sets on fire the entire course of our existence with the fire that comes to it from hell itself. Human beings can tame and have tamed all other creatures – wild animals and birds, reptiles and fish. But no one has ever been able to tame the tongue. It is evil and uncontrollable, full of deadly poison.

We use it to give thanks to our Lord and Father and also to curse other people, who are created in the likeness of God. Words of thanksgiving and cursing pour out from the same mouth. My brothers and sisters, this should not happen! No spring of water pours out sweet water and bitter water from the same opening. A fig tree, my brothers and sisters, cannot bear olives; a grapevine cannot bear figs, nor can a salty spring produce sweet water.

FROM THE LETTER OF JAMES, CHAPTER 3

121

Live in the Light

Images of darkness and light run through the New Testament. John uses this simple but strong image to great effect. The second part of the passage makes a blunt statement about self-deception and shows the way to true forgiveness.

This then is the message which we have heard of him, and declare unto you, that God is light, and in him is no darkness at all. If we say that we have fellowship with him, and walk in darkness, we lie, and do not the truth: but if we walk in the light, as he is in the light, we have fellowship one with another, and the blood of Jesus Christ his Son cleanseth us from all sin.

If we say that we have no sin, we deceive ourselves, and the truth is not in us. If we confess our sins, he is faithful and just to forgive us our sins, and to cleanse us from all unrighteousness. If we say that we have not sinned, we make him a liar, and his word is not in us.

FROM THE FIRST LETTER OF JOHN, CHAPTER 1

I WILL COME IN

Perhaps the most famous illustration of this passage is Holman Hunt's painting 'The Light of the World' in Keble College, Oxford. Christ stands outside the door, and knocks. He does not force his way in, but waits for the door to be opened. Once invited in, he shares in the life of the householder.

'And to the angel of the church in Laodicea write: The words of the Amen, the faithful and true witness, the origin of God's creation: "I know your works; you are neither cold nor hot. I wish that you were either cold or hot. So, because you are lukewarm, and neither cold nor hot, I am about to spit you out of my mouth.

'"For you say, 'I am rich, I have prospered, and I need nothing.' You do not realize that you are wretched, pitiable, poor, blind, and naked.

'"Therefore I counsel you to buy from me gold refined by fire so that you may be rich; and white robes to clothe you and to keep the shame of your nakedness from being seen; and salve to anoint your eyes so that you may see. I reprove and discipline those whom I love. Be earnest, therefore, and repent.

'"Listen! I am standing at the door, knocking; if you hear my voice and open the door, I will come in to you and eat with you, and you with me. To the one who conquers I will give a place with me on my throne, just as I myself conquered and sat down with my Father on his throne." Let anyone who has an ear listen to what the Spirit is saying to the churches.'

FROM THE BOOK OF REVELATION, CHAPTER 3

123

THE BLOOD OF THE LAMB

*The book of Revelation, written at a time of increasing
persecution, is unlike any other New Testament book.
It is 'apocalyptic' literature, full of symbols, picture
language and visions. This extract paints a picture of
a world with no evil, and the Lamb (Jesus) in the
midst of his people.*

After this I looked, and there was an enormous crowd – no one could count all the people! They were from every race, tribe, nation, and language, and they stood in front of the throne and of the Lamb, dressed in white robes and holding palm branches in their hands. They called out in a loud voice: 'Salvation comes from our God, who sits on the throne, and from the Lamb!'

All the angels stood round the throne, the elders, and the four living creatures. Then they threw themselves face downwards in front of the throne and worshipped God, saying, 'Amen! Praise, glory, wisdom, thanksgiving, honour, power, and might belong to our God for ever and ever! Amen!'

One of the elders asked me, 'Who are these people dressed in white robes, and where do they come from?'

'I don't know, sir. You do,' I answered. He said to me, 'These are the people who have come safely through the terrible persecution. They have washed their robes and made them white with the blood of the Lamb.

'That is why they stand before God's throne and serve him day and night in his temple. He who sits on the throne will protect them with his presence.

'Never again will they hunger or thirst; neither sun nor any scorching heat will burn them, because the Lamb, who is in the centre of the throne, will be their shepherd, and he will guide them to springs of life-giving water. And God will wipe away every tear from their eyes.'

FROM THE BOOK OF REVELATION, CHAPTER 7

Heaven and Earth Renewed

The last book in the Bible ends not with destruction, but with a new creation, freed from the blight of sin and death. God lives amongst his people, who can now enjoy the freedom of perfect relationships. All the glorious goodness of the Garden of Eden is recalled – but this new creation is for ever.

Then I saw a new heaven and a new earth; for the first heaven and the first earth had passed away, and the sea was no more. And I saw the holy city, the new Jerusalem, coming down out of heaven from God, prepared as a bride adorned for her husband.

And I heard a loud voice from the throne saying, 'See, the home of God is among mortals. He will dwell with them; they will be his peoples, and God himself will be with them; he will wipe every tear from their eyes. Death will be no more; mourning and crying and pain will be no more, for the first things have passed away.'

And the one who was seated on the throne said, 'See, I am making all things new.' Also he said, 'Write this, for these words are trustworthy and true.' Then he said to me, 'It is done! I am the Alpha and the Omega, the beginning and the end. To the thirsty I will give water as a gift from the spring of the water of life. Those who conquer will inherit these things, and I will be their God and they will be my children...

I saw no temple in the city, for its temple is the Lord God the Almighty and the Lamb. And the city has no need of sun or moon

126

to shine on it, for the glory of God is its light, and its lamp is the Lamb. The nations will walk by its light, and the kings of the earth will bring their glory into it. Its gates will never be shut by day – and there will be no night there. People will bring into it the glory and the honour of the nations. But nothing unclean will enter it, nor anyone who practises abomination or falsehood, but only those who are written in the Lamb's book of life.

FROM THE BOOK OF REVELATION, CHAPTER 21

ACKNOWLEDGMENTS

Extracts on pages 12, 15, 17, 24, 34, 40, 41, 51, 52, 61, 64, 65, 76, 79, 82, 83, 92, 95, 106, 112, 120 and 122 are taken from the Authorized Version of the Bible (The King James Bible), the rights of which are vested in the Crown, and are reproduced by permission of the Crown's Patentee, Cambridge University Press.

Extracts on pages 20, 30, 36, 68 and 88 are taken from the Revised English Bible © 1989 Oxford and Cambridge University Presses.

Extracts on pages 22, 28, 29, 42, 44, 45, 49, 58, 59, 69, 73, 77, 86, 90, 97, 99, 104, 114, 121 and 124 are taken from the Good News Bible published by the Bible Societies/HarperCollins Publishers Ltd UK © American Bible Society, 1966, 1971,1976, 1992.

Extracts on pages 25, 26, 32, 33, 38, 47, 53, 55, 56, 57, 70, 71, 74, 81, 84, 85, 91, 93, 100, 102, 108, 110, 115, 117, 123 and 126 are taken from the New Revised Standard Version of the Bible, Anglicized edition, copyright © 1989, 1995 by the Division of Christian Education of the National Council of Churches of Christ in the USA.

Extracts on pages 72 and 78 are taken from the New Jerusalem Bible © 1985 Darton, Longman and Todd Ltd and Doubleday and Company, Inc.

Extract on page 119 is taken from the HOLY BIBLE, NEW INTERNATIONAL VERSION. Copyright © 1973, 1978, 1984 by International Bible Society, Hodder and Stoughton Ltd. All rights reserved. 'NIV' is a registered trademark of International Bible Society. UK trademark number 1448790.